T0156528

Fair to Fabulous
in Fifteen Minutes

Your Personal Journey to a More Inspirational Life

Wayne L. Rickman

Fair to Fabulous in Fifteen Minutes
Your Personal Journey to a More Inspirational Life

Copyright © 2014 Wayne L. Rickman.

All rights reserved. No part of this book may be used or reproduced by any means, graphic, electronic, or mechanical, including photocopying, recording, taping or by any information storage retrieval system without the written permission of the publisher except in the case of brief quotations embodied in critical articles and reviews.

iUniverse books may be ordered through booksellers or by contacting:

iUniverse LLC
1663 Liberty Drive
Bloomington, IN 47403
www.iuniverse.com
1-800-Authors (1-800-288-4677)

Because of the dynamic nature of the Internet, any web addresses or links contained in this book may have changed since publication and may no longer be valid. The views expressed in this work are solely those of the author and do not necessarily reflect the views of the publisher, and the publisher hereby disclaims any responsibility for them.

Any people depicted in stock imagery provided by Thinkstock are models, and such images are being used for illustrative purposes only. Certain stock imagery © Thinkstock.

ISBN: 978-1-4917-4226-6 (sc)
ISBN: 978-1-4917-4228-0 (hc)
ISBN: 978-1-4917-4227-3 (e)

Library of Congress Control Number: 2014913715

Printed in the United States of America.

iUniverse rev. date: 10/8/2014

"It's not what we do once in a while that shapes
our lives, but what we do consistently"

Tony Robbins

"Nothing is impossible as the word itself says 'I'm possible'!"

Audrey Hepburn

"As a man thinketh in his heart so is he"

Proverbs 23:7

Contents

Part One

What Makes a Fabulous Life?

Introduction

How do you feel? Right now, as you are reading these words, how do you feel? You might be thinking, "I feel fine, Wayne. I just started reading this book." Or, you might say, "I'm okay. I'm a little tired and things aren't going so well." But I'll bet that only a few of you answered, "I am FABULOUS!" To the ones who are anything less than fabulous right now, I want to ask, "Why?" Why are you settling for a life that is anything less than a fabulous life? Do you wake up each day filled with enthusiasm and passion for the day? Do you look forward to the future while being grateful for everything you have presently? If not, why not?

My name is Wayne Rickman and I am fabulous! And, even though I don't know you, I know how to help you to become fabulous, too.

I have spent my entire professional life in sales and marketing—in areas from a sales associate to a regional VP of sales. These all require the ability to deal with rejection and maintain positivity in all situations. I was the vice president of sales and marketing for one of the most successful resort S&M teams in Virginia. Over 20 plus years there, we helped recruit and train the staff to generate what has been estimated over half a billion dollars in net sales revenue. Clearly, I couldn't do that unless I was able to lead by example and then ultimately mentor the staff on how to rebirth themselves from fair to "fabulous." At my next stop, we went on to help guide our senior leadership team at Starwood Resorts to win numerous awards both in sales performance and community service in SC. I tell you this, not in the way of bragging at all, but to illustrate how powerful the correct positive mental mindset can be. When you see yourself as fabulous, you BECOME fabulous, and life opens many more opportunities for you. Today I have been blessed with the best job yet in my career as a site VP S&M for a company voted one of Fortune magazines' most admired companies. My current duties hold me accountable for approximately 375 sales/marketing associates and $115,000,000+ in S&M revenue. Seeking the perfect mind set is a daily responsibility in this role, I am grateful for the opportunity.

Sales like the great American pastime Baseball are both filled with failure. Many times I find similarities in each that are undeniable. For example in sales when you do not make a sale you must have a short memory and flush the experience to help reset yourself to have the perfect mental mindset for your next opportunity. In baseball when you strike out you simply cannot focus on that at bat you must flush it away so once again you create the perfect competitive state of mind for your next opportunity at the plate. All our lives we experience various levels of failure or lack of success or disappointment and we will need to know how to let the water under the bridge go and focus on the things we can control. Many individuals that have played a high level of competitive sports have very successful careers in business because they have learned over the years that once an event has passed us by we need to flush those thoughts and move forward. I once watched a collegiate player strike out in the 9th inning with the winning run on 3rd base. He could have let it crush him as he came back up with the game tied in the 12th inning and hit the ball off the wall for a walk off win. That is a perfect example of corrective mindset.

Before my career, of course, I was raised by parents who may not have put in writing what you will see, read, and absorb today, but they taught me these things through their actions. So I dedicate these words of positivity to my parents, to my wife Jackie who has supported me for 3+ decades, and our two sons Joshua and Jarrod. I pray my children have the same effect on others as my father had on me and that I have tried to have on them as they grew up in our home.

No one said that life is fair and we all get tested; we all have good times and tough times. I am writing this book 3-4 plus years after I had a double heart stint placed in my heart. I am reminded of how blessed/ grateful I am to be alive today. I could have been one of the people who focused on asking, "Why Me?" But instead I choose to focus on what a fabulous life I have. After all, I almost didn't have much time with my family left at all...

Who is this book for? There are three kinds of people in life and this book can help any one of them. First, there is the person who is already living and pursuing a fabulous life. For this person, the book can help reaffirm what they already know, can give them some new tips and techniques, and can provide general inspiration.

Second, there are the readers who may be on the fence. Sure, they've seen Tony Robbins and have read and listened to motivational programs and books. But, they're still not sure whether or not this is all a bunch of "rah rah nonsense." Can personal development really change your life? This group would love to be fabulous more often and may not know how to get there.

Finally, there is what I like to call the "personal development atheist." This is the person who really doesn't believe that they can have a fabulous life. Perhaps someone gave them this book as a gift or they picked it up to see what all the fuss was about. But the personal development atheist thinks that life happens as it happens and the best you can do is accept it.

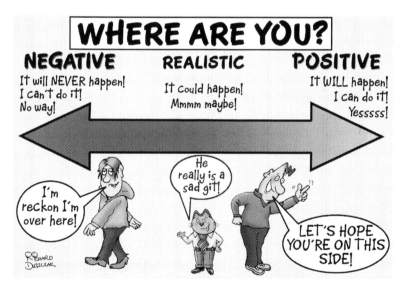

This book is for "all three" kinds of people. Of course the people in the first group already understand what it's like to have a fabulous life as it is not about the destination but how we feel on along that journey. The readers that are currently on the fence will learn some new ideas and practice some exercises that can show them how to transform their lives from fair to fabulous. And the third group, if they keep an open mind, can start to shift their thinking and dramatically improve their lives. But to do so you must have faith to experience our ideas. Not everything is this book will be a perfect fit for everyone. To have the right frame of mind focus on what you connect within the chapters to follow. My goal is to Pay It Forward to you.

I've arranged this book into two parts. The first part will give you the knowledge and understanding you need to change your life. The second part will then have you actually APPLY what you've learned. There are exercises throughout, and you have to actually DO them in order to change your life. You can't just read about doing sit-ups and expect to get six pack abs, can you? For some the toughest parts of exercise, be it mental or physical, is getting started so do one at a time and setup a milestone or completion date so you have a goal in place to finish each step.

One Last Thing

Perhaps the most important piece of advice I can give you as you start this process is to be gentle with yourself. There are going to be frustrating times in your life when things aren't progressing as rapidly as you'd like. We humans are impatient creatures! Don't fall into the trap of binary thinking. You know what this is. On/Off, Succeed/Fail, Winner/Loser. Brian Tracy likes to say, "All you have to do is improve 1/10th of 1% every day, and you will succeed." Earl Nightingale puts it this way, "Success is the progression toward a worthy goal." *Body for Life* star Bill Phillips says, "Progress not perfection". As long as you are moving forward, you are succeeding. Be kind to yourself. You have the rest of your life to do this.

Ask anyone of age that has been very successful and they will tell you each probably has had an 800 square foot home and a 5800 square foot home. Some have been blessed enough to have had a Fiat all the way to a Ferrari. Others have had $1,000 in the bank $10,000 or $100,000 or even a $1,000,000. But none of the above guarantees you will have a Fabulous life. Throughout this book you will see that happiness is definitely internal not external.

This will be a fun, easy to read journey so complete the book first and then find the chapters or the quotes or the exercises that seem to find a place in improving your life. The key is to get started and then stay committed and refer to it often as you create an improved mindset.

Are you ready to get started, do you have the perfect mindset to read the rest of this book. There are many opportunities for personal and professional improvement. But like a parachute the mind operates best only when open. So if you are ready let us start with Chapter One.

Chapter One:

How to Create a Crystal Clear Vision (or, Clean Off Your Glasses)

"All our dreams can come true, if we have the courage to pursue them."

-Walt Disney-

How many of you have ever been to Disneyland? Most people reading this probably have been to the "Magical Kingdom" at least once in their lives.

The first time I went to Disneyland, I wandered around aimlessly, amazed by the sights and sounds. I stood in line for two hours to go on one ride, and then wandered to the other side of the park to stand in an equally long line for another ride. At the end of my twelve-hour day, I'd only gone on four rides.

Later in my life, I discovered a "guidebook" to Disneyland, with several potential itineraries, depending on what kinds of rides you wanted to go on. There was an itinerary for families with small children, one for adults, and one for teenagers. It gave specific advice as to which rides had the longest lines, and which were popular at different times of the day. Never again did I waste my day at Disneyland, wandering from ride to ride, missing out on things I wanted to do.

This book is just like that. Sure, you can jump right into the action and start exercising and managing your time better. But, unless you have an overall vision for where you are going with this program, you're not going to make the most of it. This program is like Disneyland in that there are more rides to go on than there is time in a day. To maximize your experience in this program, you're going to have to get focused on which are the most important areas for you, personally, to improve.

To get a clear vision for your life, we are going to start really huge. In the following space, write down the top ten things you want to do in your lifetime. Think big! Want to start a charity? How about going on a safari? Perhaps your biggest goal is to find the perfect mate, marry, and have children. Whatever your dreams are, write them here. Don't get sidetracked with whether or not these dreams are realistic. This is the really big picture here.

Sometimes these are referred to as a BHAG, big hairy aggressive goals. Everyone should have some BHAG's in their lives. This is an excellent time for you to start yours.

> **"As long as you are going to think anyway—
> you might as well think BIG!"**
>
> **Donald Trump**

In the book *What They Don't Teach You in the Harvard Business School,* Mark McCormack tells a study conducted on students in the 1979 Harvard MBA program. In that year, the students were asked, "Have you set clear, written goals for your future and made plans to accomplish them?" Only 3 percent of the graduates had written goals and plans; 13 percent had goals, but they were not in writing; and a whopping 84 percent had no specific goals at all.

Ten years later, the members of the class were interviewed again, and the findings, while somewhat predictable, were nonetheless astonishing. The 13 percent of the class who had goals were earning, on average, twice as much as the 84 percent who had no goals at all. Then what about the three percent who had clear, written goals? They were earning, on average, **Ten Times as much as the other 97 percent put together!** What can you learn from this group?

In spite of such proof of success, most people don't have clear, measurable, time-bounded goals that they work toward daily. So we are going to help you get started right now, make the commitment. Remember it all starts with our thoughts something we can control every night just before we go to bed and every day as soon as we wake up. Some do not have goals because they believe they are unachievable, you must believe you can do way more than you are doing today.

Write some of your goals on note pad and place them where you have easy access. Use the mirror in your bedroom, the visor in your car, the desk at your office. Give yourself as much positive daily re-enforcement as possible. It really does work and you will greatly benefit but you must start right now as any goals are better than no goals at all, stop now and get started. Where is your current mindset and is it going to help you get further away or closer to your goal?

Seven Things I Want to Do In My Lifetime

1. _____

2. _____

3. _____

4. _____

5. _____

6. _____

7. _____

There. How does that look? "It looks great, Wayne, but what does this have to do with the fifteen minutes. Obviously you're not telling me that I can achieve these in fifteen minutes!" What we need you to start doing is commit to fifteen minutes a day towards your goals. That can only be accomplished by spending fifteen minutes every day for an attitude adjustment or as Zig Ziglar used to say so successfully, "Give yourself a check-up from the neck-up." Many people write goals and place them in a drawer and review them only at the end of the year and others leave them there and basically forget them. You need to make the choice that you want these things to happen and you are willing to do whatever it takes to get them done.

While anything is possible, there is a different reason for writing down your dream list. This list will tell you a lot about yourself and which things you should pick to work on. Are most of the goals physical? "I want to climb Mount Everest." Maybe the goals are relationship oriented. "I want to have five children." Some people choose financial goals. "I want to make ten million dollars." Some could be athletic/academic goals, "I want to hit .300 and make the Dean's List." Few ever think about having specific mindset or attitude goals, have you?

In the following spaces, write down the categories that the above goals fit into. You'll probably find that they fit into categories like career, relationships, physical, financial, spiritual, educational, personal, hobby, sports, et cetera.

These are the categories my goals fit into:

1) _____
2) _____
3) _____
4) _____
5) _____

Now, how many did you have in each category? Was there one category that had more goals than the others? If so, that's your primary area to work on. Were they pretty equally distributed? If so, then you're going to have to prioritize which order you want to work on them in. Rearrange them by ranking them in the order of importance to you.

It's a good idea to mostly focus mostly on two or three goals at a time. Any more than that and you will be diluting your efforts. Change is hard, and your mind is going to fight you on it, so you need to be able to develop some serious momentum by focusing your attention on a few good goals. We'll talk more about how to set a good goal in a later chapter, but for now, just understand that you can really only effectively change two or three things at a time. You can actually change your whole life around this way. I did. But, personal growth is an ongoing process. You never get "there" even when you achieve all of the things on that list above, you're still not going to be "there" because you will have newer, better goals to work on then. So, slow down, take it easy, and change only two or three things at a time. All start first with your mindset

Here are the three categories I'd like to change:

1) _____
2) _____
3) _____

The Magic Wand Exercise

This is a classic coaching exercise that coaches use to help clients define their ideal life. This is different from the exercise above in that it's not identifying the big, lofty lifetime goals, but is instead identifying a "regular day".

In the space below, answer the following question. "If I had a magic wand, and could make my life perfect tomorrow, how would it look?" Describe your perfect day *within the life you already have.* In other words, you can't say that you're married to Tom Cruise (unless you really are) or that you've won the lottery. You have to use your real spouse, your actual children, and the home you are living in now. This might be harder than you anticipate, because it's so easy to think of some fantasy life that doesn't exist, but is much harder to think of ways to improve the life you already have. Write your thoughts here, and be sure to include the categories you created above.

If I had a magic wand and could wake up tomorrow with the perfect life it would be:

Okay, now we are getting somewhere! You've got some big picture huge lifetime goals, and you've created some categories for change or improvement. You've also created a great description or mission of the perfect life for you. I'll bet your vision is already a whole lot clearer than when you started this chapter. We have a long way to go, but we can get there.

Where there is no Vision, the people perish.

-Proverbs 29:18-

But what is critical is that you start and that you do so right now. Reading this book is an excellent first step. Please read it often, at least 15 minutes a day. You will see very quickly that once you set your mind to something you can effect change and much quicker than you thought.

What's next then? Is it time to jump in and start working on these goals? Not even close. Using my Disneyland example, all we've done so far is get an idea of what rides we want to go on. We're still missing a lot of information. In order to make these goals into reality, we need to take a look at the process of change. This starts with each and every page in this book, but before we talk about physical results we must focus on the mental side of goal setting and achieving.

Chapter One Summary

Before you can create a Fair to Fabulous Life; you must first find your personal road map for success. What are your goals in life? What are your dreams? Where do you see yourself in the next year, five years, ten years, etc.? How does the future look, bright? The design of your personal road map towards a Fabulous Life requires taking the temperature of your innermost morals, feelings, goals, hopes and dreams; yet, few ever take the time to identify these important aspects of a fabulous life. YOU can be the beacon that guides others in changing the world from fair to fabulous! Empowering, isn't it? Stop at the end of this chapter and get started.

When thinking about setting your own personal goals, consider the competitors of a track and field event. The runner has the future – the race – in mind and has developed a strategy for completing the challenge. You have the desire for a fabulous life, just as the runner has a roadmap for completing the race. Identifying your goals, hopes and dreams is similar to the starting line of a track and field event. Once identified, you'll have a clear direction for where your life is headed and what you wish to achieve. As your personal road map continues to take shape, you will inch closer and closer to your finish line: that of living a Fabulous Life!

Just as a Disneyland guidebook is filled with itineraries to help visitors navigate the facility, filled with categories tailored to a guests' interests, categorizing your personal goals by those that most interest or can best benefit you will help you to begin traveling the road from Fair to Fabulous! Many financial analysts in their debt reducing strategies discuss how paying off a small debt is better at the start of a debt reduction plan than diving head first into a massive debt. Why? Because eliminating smaller debt first can provide a sense of accomplishment that fuels an individual's long-term goals of living debt free. The same is true for those choosing to live a fabulous life. Maybe, for you, accomplishing a few smaller goals on your list will fuel your inner passion to strive for bigger and better things. Think big, but start small, making a simple commitment to follow this journey for fifteen minutes each and every day until doing so becomes a habit, a healthy habit that brings you closer to a fabulous life ahead!

Chapter Two:

Mental Mindset Management

**"Nothing can stop the man with the right mental attitude;
Nothing can help the man with the wrong mental attitude."**

-Thomas Jefferson-

What is your first impression when you read this and what does this quote mean to you? How did he know this so very long ago? Clearly, the benefits of his words have been around for a long time and yet so many people fail to live by them. Your own mental mindset (attitude) is the main difference between success and failure, between having a fair life and a fabulous one. So, in order to have a fabulous life, you need to learn how to manage your thinking.

**"The happiness of your life depends on
the quality of your thoughts;
therefore guard yours accordingly."**

-Marcus Aurelius-

How could people have discovered this so long ago and so many not know it today? What is the quality of your thoughts? Do you think the best or worst when a challenge presents itself? Recite this simple phrase, or print it and tape it where you can see it every day/week.

You have to manage your thoughts as your thoughts become your words.

You have to pay attention to your words as your words become your actions.

You have to monitor your actions as repeating them they become your habits.

You have to work hard on creating the right habits as they define your character.

You have to develop your character as ultimately character determines your destiny.

Or if you prefer we have rearranged the meaning in a simple readable format:

Today I know begins with each and every "thought";
I am going to be optimistic as nothing will make me distraught.
Please be the wind beneath my wings so I can fly high like a bird,
By being extremely attentive to what I say with each and every "word".
When confronted I need to be careful to respond and not have a reaction,
For what quickly crosses my lips will ultimately be put right into "action".

When my positivity rules the day it can and will multiply just like rabbits,
As these things we say/do/feel ultimately become our personal "habits".
In the long run these daily efforts will pay off of that I am very sure,
As responding to life's challenges will always build upon my "character".
I know it takes work and will take a great deal of extra effort from me,
But in the end this daily discipline will become my mental "destiny".

Wayne L. Rickman
April 26, 2013

Ph.D. in Positivity

If I could, I would have awarded my father with an honorary Ph.D. in Positivity as he has the amazing ability to find something good in everyone and everything. Whenever anyone asks him 'how are you today,' he gives the same answer? I am just south of great! Having a great attitude was a daily goal of his and saying he is just south means as good as it is it still needs work. This was especially true in the later years of his life. You need to see and remember that we do get to "choose" every day what our frame of mind is in every situation. No matter how educated or uneducated you may be - no matter how old or how young you may be - to succeed in life at any level consistently must instill in yourself this fundamental DNA. What are you doing every single day to make certain you have the best possible mental mindset? It does not come easy, it takes a great deal of personal discipline, but I promise once you get to fabulous you will never want to go back as everything is life will smell, taste, and feel better when positive.

Defining success is important, but taking a clear-eyed look at the impact of your personal definition matters even more. As in most things your intent is important but the end results provide the real answers to how we can all become more fabulous every day.

If helping others through social work is your personal definition of success, for example, you may make a decent living but you won't get rich... and you must embrace that fact. If you're happy, you have and that is all that really matters.

If building a $100 million company is your definition of success, you can have a family but it will be almost improbable to have a rich, full engaged family life as success has a price... and you must embrace that fact. If you're happy, you have. So forget traditional definitions of success. Forget what other people think/say. Ask yourself if you feel happy -- not just at work, not just at home, not just in those fleeting moments when you do something just for yourself, but overall. If you are, you're successful. The happier you are the more successful you are.

If you aren't happy it's time to rethink how you define success, and start making changes to your professional and personal life that align with that definition, because what you're doing now isn't working for you. And life is way too short for that.

What does success mean to you? Not some general textbook or online definition of success. If asked what do you and your family life look like when you are successful? Have you yet developed a strong written vision statement of what you will look like when you are truly successful? This will help you step into becoming that person in your imagination's shoes. When you do then and only then you will start living life as a success. You need to know where you are going in order to ever get there. This becomes your personal GPS. How can you ever get there is you have not written vision of what and where getting there means to you? Just Do It...

I highly recommend you stop now and write your own vision statement. If you do not know how, just Google the words "vision statement" and see what others have done. Then take that template and write one for yourself, when done place it somewhere that you can see it.

Now you have your GPS that you can refer to in much less than 15 minutes a day. If you commit to mental mindset management at least 15 minutes a day this is when the odds shift in your favor and you are on your own personal journey from Fair to Fabulous.

The Legacy Exercise

As a simple exercise, take time to write at least 5-8 lines on how you would like to be remembered at your job or with your kids, with your significant other, or at your job after your departure. This sort of obituary will be a difficult task and may take several drafts. This is a very personal exercise and can be done by asking yourself. What is the difference between the person you want to be and the person that other people see? When you write down how you want to be remembered or discussed after your departure then you can work on becoming that person every day. Once complete, once totally satisfied that is how you would like to be remembered then print it and place it somewhere you can see it and plant those thoughts every day so that this new vision can now become your reality. It's like a daily goal of who you want to become...

How I Want to Be Remembered:

_____
_____
_____
_____
_____
_____

"I would like to be remembered as someone who accomplished useful deeds, and who was a kind and loving person. I would like to leave the memory of a human being with a correct attitude and who did her best to help others."

-Grace Kelly-

If the words above are who you'd like to become, what are you doing daily to make it happen? Leaving a legacy is something you do not with your words but with your actions. Each and every day we get the choice, regardless of what happened yesterday, how to embrace today.

Earl Nightingale wrote an article on "The Strangest Secret."[1]

The Strangest Secret

Some years ago, the late Nobel prize-winning Dr. Albert Schweitzer was asked by a reporter, "Doctor, what's wrong with men today?" The great doctor was silent a moment, and then he said, "Men simply don't think!"

It's about this that I want to talk with you. We live today in a golden age. This is an era that humanity has looked forward to, dreamed of, and worked toward for thousands of years. We live in the richest era that ever existed on the face of the earth ... a land of abundant opportunity for everyone.

However, if you take one hundred individuals at the age of twenty five, do you have any idea what will happen to those men and women by the time they're sixty five? These one hundred people all believe they're going to be successful. They are eager toward life, there is a certain sparkle in their eye, a confidence to their carriage, and life seems like a pretty interesting adventure to them.

---

[1] http://www.nightingale.com/ae_article-i-22-article-strangestsecret.aspx

But by the time they're 65, only one will be rich, four will be financially independent, five will still be working, and 54 will be broke — depending on others for life's necessities.

Only five out of 100 make the grade! Why do so many fail? What has happened to the sparkle that was there when they were 25? What has become of the dreams, the hopes, the plans ... and why is there such a large disparity between what these people intended to do and what they actually accomplished?

THE DEFINITION OF SUCCESS

First, we have to define success and here is the best definition I've ever been able to find: "Success is the progressive realization of a worthy ideal."

A success is the school teacher who is teaching because that's what he or she wants to do. A success is the entrepreneur who starts his own company because that was his dream — that's what he wanted to do. A success is the salesperson who wants to become the best salesperson in his or her company and sets forth on the pursuit of that goal.

A success is anyone who is realizing a worthy predetermined ideal, because that's what he or she decided to do ... deliberately. But only one out of 20 does that! The rest are "failures."

Rollo May, the distinguished psychiatrist, wrote a wonderful book called Man's Search for Himself, and in this book he says: "The opposite of courage in our society is not cowardice ... it is conformity." And there you have the reason for so many failures. Conformity — people acting like everyone else, without knowing why or where they are going.

We learn to read by the time we're seven. We learn to make a living by the time we're 30. Often by that time we're not only making a living, we're supporting a family. And yet by the time we're 65, we haven't learned how to become financially independent in the richest land that has ever been known. Why? We conform! Most of us are acting like the wrong percentage group — the 95 who don't succeed.

GOALS

Have you ever wondered why so many people work so hard and honestly without ever achieving anything in particular, and why others don't seem to work hard, yet seem to get everything? They seem to have the "magic touch." You've heard people say, "Everything he touches turns to gold." Have you ever noticed that a person who becomes successful tends to continue to become more successful? And, on the other hand, have you noticed how someone who's a failure tends to continue to fail?

The difference is goals. People with goals succeed because they know where they're going. It's that simple. Failures, on the other hand, believe that their lives are shaped by circumstances ... by things that happen to them ... by exterior forces.

Think of a ship with the complete voyage mapped out and planned. The captain and crew know exactly where the ship is going and how long it will take — it has a definite goal. And 9,999 times out of 10,000, it will get there.

Now let's take another ship — just like the first — only let's not put a crew on it, or a captain at the helm. Let's give it no aiming point, no goal, and no destination. We just start the engines and let it go. I think you'll agree that if it gets out of the harbor at all, it will either sink or wind up on some deserted beach — a derelict. It can't go anyplace because it has no destination and no guidance.

It's the same with a human being. However, the human race is fixed, not to prevent the strong from winning, but to prevent the weak from losing. Society today can be likened to a convoy in time of war. Society can be slowed down to protect its weakest link, just as the naval convoy has to go at the speed that will permit its slowest vessel to remain in formation.

That could be why so many make such a modest living today. It takes no special drive or desire to make a minimum wage living. Thus some have a plateau of so-called "security." So, to succeed, all we must do is decide how high above this plateau we want to aim.

Throughout history, the great wise men and teachers, philosophers, and prophets have disagreed with one another on many different things. It is only on this one point that they are in complete and unanimous agreement, the key to success and the key to failure is this:

WE BECOME WHAT WE THINK ABOUT

This is The Strangest Secret! Now, why do I say it's strange, and why do I call it a secret? Actually, it isn't a secret at all. It was first promulgated by some of the earliest wise men, and it appears again and again throughout the Bible. But very few people have learned it or understand it. That's why it's strange, and why for some equally strange reason it virtually remains a secret.

Marcus Aurelius, the great Roman Emperor, said: "A man's life is what his thoughts make of it."

Disraeli said this: "Everything comes if a man will only wait ... a human being with a settled purpose must accomplish it, and nothing can resist a will that will stake even existence for its fulfillment."

William James said: "We need only in cold blood act as if the thing in question were real, and it will become infallibly real by growing into such a connection with our life that it will become real. It will become so knit with habit and emotion that our interests in it will be those which characterize belief." He continues, "... only you must, then, really wish these things, and wish them exclusively, and not wish at the same time a hundred other incompatible things just as strongly."

Dr. Norman Vincent Peale put it this way: "If you think in negative terms, you will get negative results. If you think in positive terms, you will achieve positive results." George Bernard Shaw said: "People are always blaming their circumstances for what they are. I don't believe in circumstances. The people who get on in this world are the people who get up and look for the circumstances they want, and if they can't find them, make them."

Well, it's pretty apparent, isn't it? We become what we think about. A person who is thinking about a concrete and worthwhile goal is going to reach it, because that's what he's thinking about. Conversely, the person who has no goal, who doesn't know where he's going, and whose thoughts must therefore be thoughts of confusion, anxiety, fear, and worry will thereby create a life of frustration, fear, anxiety and worry. And if he thinks about nothing ... he becomes nothing.

<u>AS YE SOW — SO SHALL YE REAP</u>

The human mind is much like a farmer's land. The land gives the farmer a choice. He may plant in that land whatever he chooses. The land doesn't care what is planted. It's up to the farmer to make the decision. The mind, like the land, will return what you plant, but it doesn't care what you plant. Thus the creation of this quote, "As ye sow, so shall ye reap."

The human mind is far more fertile, far more incredible and mysterious than the land, but it works the same way. It doesn't care what we plant ... success ... or failure. A concrete, worthwhile goal ... or confusion, misunderstanding, fear, anxiety, and so on. But what we plant it must return to us. The problem is that our mind comes as standard equipment at birth. It's free. And things that are given to us for nothing, we place little value on. Things that we pay money for or work hard to get, we value more.

The paradox is that exactly the reverse is true. Everything that's really worthwhile in life came to us free — our minds, our souls, our bodies, our hopes, our dreams, our ambitions, our intelligence, our love of family and children and friends and country. All these priceless possessions are free.

But the things that cost us money are actually very cheap and can be replaced at any time. A good man can be completely wiped out and make another fortune. He can do that several times. Even if our home burns down, we can rebuild it. But the things we got for nothing, we can never replace.

Our mind can do any kind of job we assign to it, but generally speaking, we use it for little jobs instead of big ones. So decide now. What is it you want? Plant your goal in your mind. It's the most important decision you'll ever make in your entire life.

Do you want to excel at your particular job? Do you want to go places in your company ... in your community? Do you want to get rich? All you have got to do is plant that seed in your mind, care for it, work steadily toward your goal, and it will become a reality.

It not only will, there's no way that it cannot. You see, that's a law — like the laws of Sir Isaac Newton, the laws of gravity. If you get on top of a building and jump off, you'll always go down — you'll never go up.

And it's the same with all the other laws of nature. They always work. They're inflexible. Think about your goal in a relaxed, positive way. Picture yourself in your mind's eye as having already achieved this goal. See yourself doing the things you will be doing when you have reached your goal.

Every one of us is the sum total of our own thoughts. We are where we are because that's exactly where we really want or feel we deserve to be — whether we'll admit that or not. Each of us must live off the fruit of our thoughts in the future, because what you think today and tomorrow — next month and next year — will mold your life and determine your future. You're guided by your mind.

I remember one time I was driving through an eastern state and I saw one of those giant earthmoving machines roaring along the road with what looked like 30 tons of dirt in it — a tremendous, incredible machine — and there was a little man perched way up on top with the wheel in his hands, guiding it. As I drove along I was struck by the similarity of that machine to the human mind. Just suppose you're sitting at the controls of such a vast source of energy. Are you going to sit back and fold your arms and let it run itself into a ditch? Or are you going to keep both hands firmly on the wheel and control and direct this power to a specific, worthwhile purpose? It's up to you. You're in the driver's seat. You see, the very law that gives us success is a double-edged sword. We must control our thinking. The same rule that can lead people to lives of success, wealth, happiness, and all the things they ever dreamed of — that very same law can lead them into the gutter. It's all in how they use it ... for good or for bad. That is The Strangest Secret!

Do what the experts since the dawn of recorded history have told us to do: pay the price, by becoming the person you want to become. It's not nearly as difficult as living unsuccessfully. Remember you must not only pay full price but you must pay in advance.

The moment you decide on a goal to work toward, you're immediately a successful person — you are then in that rare group of people who know where they're going. Out of every hundred people, you belong to the top five. Don't concern yourself too much with how you are going to achieve your goal — leave that completely to a power greater than yourself. All you have to do is know where you're going. The answers will come to you of their own accord, and at the right time.

Start today. You have nothing to lose — but you have your whole life to win.

The Strangest Secret is a powerful concept that can help you shift your life from fair to fabulous. You see, it's about learning to reframe the "bad" circumstances in life. Let's try an example.

In the following space, identify a negative circumstance you are currently facing.

_____

_____

_____

_____

_____

Next, ask yourself, "How can I see or frame this situation differently?" Write your answer in the following space.

_____

_____

_____

_____

_____

Ever wonder why so many people today jump to conclusions and think so negatively before taking time to review their circumstance? We do not have many choices today but we can choose how we react or respond to every given situation. For example imagine you were sick and you went to your doctor and he said, "I'll give you a shot to help you." Then during your follow-up appointment he says, "You are having a bad reaction to the medication," is that positive or negative? Of course any reaction that is going to have a negative effect on your body is not good and in this case it's your mental state of mind. So if you went back for that same follow-up appointment and the doctor said, "You are responding wonderfully to that medication," is that positive or negative? Of course a responding means you are getting better and your feeling more positive. What can you do to step back and think before you reply? How can we apply this to your life every day moving forward so you are more responsive and not so reactive? It will take work as old habits die-hard, so keep this quote handy, and refer to it often. There is a substantial difference between reacting and responding to each challenge we encounter and we must remember that the choice is always ours to make each day.

> **"What happens is not as important as
> how you react to what happens."**
>
> **-Thaddeus Golas-**

The next time you have a "storm" in your personal, professional, or athletic life and you have an emotional response, ask yourself. Am I responding to this challenge, or am I reacting? We all have storms, we all encounter adversity; we all have challenges and difficulties, why then are the results so different? Each of these will teach us that when you learn to better manage your mental mindset by reframing negative circumstances, you are on your way to a fabulous life!

As a quick sports analogy in baseball, for example, the better players work hard on developing the skills to run faster, to throw more accurately, on fielding ground balls, or hitting a round ball with a round bat that is coming at them at 90+ miles per hour. They even refer to some elite players as having all 5 tools needed to succeed. But a great friend of mine that is a pro scout said there are really 6 tools; the last one being makeup or mindset management. They work hours and hours on the physical tools and even spend thousands of dollars on private lessons and equipment to give them an edge. Yet few spend enough time at all on the mental game that will really ultimately determine their success. What a shame to have God-given gifts of speed or athleticism but your mind can prevent succeeding to the maximum of your ability.

My cardiologist says I need to ride an exercise bike 5 nights weekly and as I desire a long fulfilling life so I take the prescriptions he has given me and ride my bike diligently. But I also know that I need brain food, positive brain food. Remember the "Storms Will Come" and you can read about them in the Bible in more detail. In our lives we will all encounter work storms, whether positional eliminations or people being promoted to a job you felt you deserve the most. Or having a boss you feel plays favorites, there are many situations that can affect you mentally speaking. Or in sports, someone in the lineup or on a team that should be you, et cetera. Thus remember this if you can, "It's never what happens, but how we choose to deal with what happens that always determines the final outcome." Your 6th tool is your mental mindset.

"Every day we wake up and just like the clothing we chose to put on we get to choose what mental mind set we will wear that day good or bad. Remember that it is the one thing in our life that no one controls but ourselves"

-Wayne L Rickman-

The most important tool you can develop is to learn how to manage the eight inches or real estate between your ears. Tapes, books, meditation, prayer, all require that you seek out opportunities to strengthen your mental muscles. What have you done recently to exercise the gift you were born with, the internal confidence required to convince you that no matter the circumstances or size that you really can do anything.

Remember to tell yourself often, today my mindset towards everything is "My Choice" and anyone that attempts to pull me down of to think otherwise today is not stronger than I am. My mind belongs to be and I am going to work every day to be stronger than the day before.

So if it is not the event but how we respond or react to that event, we really can take control of our lives and especially our daily mental mindset. Sometimes you just have to say, "Stop it" to yourself and make those negative thoughts go away. For example when your computer is not working and you call the hotline for help what is the first thing they ask you to do. Yes they will say reboot or turn it off clearing the memory and start over with a fresh slate. Do you "reboot" yourself? How do you shake off a bad attitude? How do you reboot your mindset? Some do it with prayer, others with meditation and for me it was tapes and books like the Secret or my favorite author like Zig Ziglar who said you need "a check-up from the neck-up". Whatever works for you is fine. But it can be done, as the one thing we are in total control of daily is our thoughts. It will take work, keep the quote above handy and refer to it often. There is also a great deal of effective information online about improving mental mindset management.

All of us have negative thoughts and negative emotions. For example a husband and wife can get along flawlessly for three weeks and then one thing goes wrong (regardless of who is at fault) and they have a big argument that can last for hours/days/weeks. What happened to the 21 straight days that everyone was outstanding? How can just one mistake become more important than the three weeks of bliss? It doesn't seem fair that 1 day can make the prior 21 go away, but no one said life is fair. So when self-doubt, when anger, or when any negative thought or emotion pops into your head, stop and say "no" or say "stop it" or even say to yourself "go away!" Reset yourself by using gratitude right then at that moment, meaning **the only way to make negative thoughts go away is by replacing them with positive thoughts.** Every Day think of the three things you are the most grateful for in your life that will bring you a smile.

Remember if someone does something amazing for you and/or your family and you do not practice gratitude, meaning you do not go out of your way to show your appreciation or acknowledge them, then in fact you are being ungrateful. That means you are taking that person or situation for granted. The opposite of gratitude is of course lacking feelings of appreciation or being ungrateful. Thus not taking the time to say thank-you can be very damaging to what is a very positive experience. Gratitude is a very powerful emotion and I highly recommend you take the online Gratitude Challenge after you complete the exercises in this book. I focus on the things I am grateful for every single day, when you are grateful your mindset is nearly perfect.

The Gratitude Challenge asks you to write down the 3-5 things you after the most grateful for you in your life before you go to bed each night. When you wake up the next day you read them and thus start the day with an Attitude of Gratitude. Rather than focusing on what you may not have at this time in your life it helps us focus and appreciate what you do have each and every day. Many such resources are available online this is one of my favorite exercises.

Why do we ask you to focus on being more grateful every day? It is pretty simple when you have negative thoughts (and we all let them sneak into our minds) the only way to make those go away is to replace them with more dominant positive thoughts. What is more positive than being grateful for your family, your friends, your health, your job, your spirituality? Some say they have little to be grateful about so remember when constructing your list the more you are grateful for the more of the same you will attract into your life. The Law of Attraction is very real and another subject you can search about online, or watch The Secret Movie. It is a thought process that has been around way longer than anyone reading this book and another way to focus on the cup being half full as opposed to those that always want to focus on the half empty part. Do Not look at or talk about what you do not have, but focus on what you do have and what you appreciate the most. We all have some many things in our lives that are a blessing, show your genuine gratitude for 30 days and before you know it your list will grow accordingly.

Changing the way you talk to yourself.

All of us have positive and negative thoughts every single day and all of us have positive or helpful self-talk and negative or destructive self-talk more than you may think. For example 'wow I look awesome in this new outfit' or 'wow I look terrible in this outfit'. Worse yet there are some that you know who if three people came up and said something less than positive about his or her clothing that day they'd want to immediately go home and change; yet if three people said something positing or inspiring about their dress would feel very confident. We must remember that self-confidence and self-doubt both come from the same person. Your inner self is what you need to realize is in complete control of your self-esteem and your self-confidence. For example, no one can make you mad or make you feel bad without your permission. If you were confident about your clothing and three people said something less than flattering you could just say 'those people just don't matter; I am very comfortable in my own skin today.'

When I dress up and wear a suit and tie I enjoy wearing nice suspenders. Why, because I like them that's why. Yet I have had some around me who say no one wears suspenders they are not in fashion any more or right now. My response, 'I like them, I enjoy them and I am wearing them because, just like the attitude I wear each day, I too get to choose the clothing I wear each day.' Wear what you want, wear what you like wear and what makes you feel good; please don't wear what you think others will like or what you feel would make you more popular.

How many of you have ever encountered less than positive self-talk? You know that person in your head encouraging or discouraging you from making choices. Self-talk comes to us in many ways like wondering if your spouse or significant other has a relationship outside your primary one. Unless you are finding lipstick or men's clothing near your wife/girlfriends personal belonging, why do you allow thoughts like that even creep into your head?

Everyone experiences self-doubt at times in their lives and to have self-confidence takes work, but once again the message remains the same: it starts with what you plant in your mind. These emotions can relax you when positive and when otherwise cause high levels of anxiety.

The stress you feel from negative self-talk is as real, as if the event had actually happened and thus we must realize the only way to make these less than positive feelings and thoughts go away is to replace them with positive or supportive self-talk. As a quick easy example, what if your own child was lacking confidence in a youth baseball game. Would you say to them? Just think of not striking out, whatever you do just don't strike out? Or would say you to them 'you can do it, you can hit the ball, I believe in you and love you. Remember that book we read to you when you were young about that little train, I think I can, I think I can, I think I can…' I know it sounds simple but phrases like 'I think I can' are a perfect example of positive self-talk.

Yes, we can help our children with positive thinking but at a much higher level sports psychology is real and it is powerful. In my research, I came across someone with multiple years of high level experience teaching positive mindset management with professional teams such as The Pittsburgh Steelers, The Dallas Cowboys, The Philadelphia Eagles, The Miami Dolphins, The New Orleans Saints, and many large successful corporations in the USA.

Dr Kevin Elko has a doctorate in Cognitive Behavioral Psychology, which means he learned how to help change the way people conduct conversations with themselves says; **"Changing the way you talk to yourself can totally revolutionize your life,** but learning how to do it can take some time and guidance."

What does this quote mean to you personally? To me, it reaffirms that everything we have discussed thus far that our life starts with our thoughts and that controlling our thoughts (self-talk) can and will help us get control of our lives. The mini-exercises in this book are meant to be but one small step in that direction as long as you set aside 15 minutes a day to reboot, like a computer. This guidance will help you make certain your personal mindset is correct for that day or moment or situation before" you open your mouth and respond.

What is the quality of your self-talk; do you help yourself or hurt yourself? You know that person that resides in your mind and daily talks you into or out of so many situations.

> **"The greatest discovery of our generation is that human beings can alter their lives by altering their attitudes of mind. As you think, so shall you be."**
>
> **-William James-**

Once again quote after quote, author after author, and historian after historian are all following this thought process. How can they possibly all be wrong, how can so many in such different parts of society and born sometimes decades apart know that we can alter our lives with something as simple as our thoughts? Because it is real and you must believe it is real. You do get to choose and the more you work at it the better you will be at managing your daily mindset.

How can all these great leaders/mentors all know this and yet so many of us were never taught? Belief starts with our thoughts, our daily thoughts. What do you believe, what do you want to believe, you can change your life right now? But not until you change your thoughts and you have the capacity to do so if you will commit to just 15 minutes a day in this book. There are no guarantees in life but we can help tilt the odds in your favor if you put in the effort up front.

In my new role I have been blessed to work alongside a mental giant. What I mean is this leader will always inspire you to simply "Impose Your Will". What he means is simple is the situation stronger or is your will to win stronger? All of us yearn to make a difference in the lives of others and in this case rarely do you ever meet a guy like Butch. You know one of those people that no matter how difficult the task, no matter how steep the hill you have to climb, no matter how impossible it may seem, he is always there to tell you that you got this task.

We should all seek that internal energizer bunny, that powerful belief the level of self-confidence that every winner in business and in sports says is where champions are born. Whom do you mentor, who needs or depends on you? It is your children, your husband/wife significant other, your friends, your employees, your employer. There are people in everyone's life that need someone to lean on and you can be that person, but it will take work.

Develop a daily regime of positive self-talk, simple positive affirmations that prepare you for each day. We all have stuff, we all experience challenge, we can all impose our will to win.

Chapter Two Summary

To embrace the goal of living a fabulous life, you must first manage your thinking. Our thoughts serve as the driving force behind every decision we make in life. More than that, whatever we are thinking – good or bad – fuels our choice of words and ultimately our actions. In keeping with the trip planning analogy from Chapter One's summary, negative self-talk and a poor attitude leads you along a path filled with bumps in the road and even the occasional pothole, should you become stuck in that way of thinking. However, positive self-talk and an optimistic mindset for the future will help to make your road to a fabulous life nothing short of smooth sailing. This is not to say bumps in the road cannot happen; life can be very unpredictable and challenges can and do arise, but the key is to accept the challenges when they come as a momentary setback and remain focused on the journey ahead. Our actions become our habits, which in turn, define our character and our character can be strengthened by the tough times you may face while pursuing your pathway to a happier, more fulfilling life.

If you choose to adopt the belief that your life, at current, is "just south of great," you will develop a greater understanding of remaining optimistic, while leaving never-ending room for personal growth. There are some that belief that life is one big learning experience, each day that we live. If you awaken each morning, grateful to be alive and make a personal affirmation to learn something new, you live a life that is just south of great. This framing of the mind encourages you to see the glass as half full and encourages a positive outlook.

Defining what success means to you will aid your forward momentum. Success to another may carry a different definition than what the term means to you and that's okay. Every person alive today is following their own journey; you only need to be focused on your personal trek to fabulous! Happiness is like gasoline in your car; it fuels your drive to a better livelihood. Your personal vision statement is your personal GPS, directing your course to a fabulous life.

Cliché as it may sound; our actions speak louder than our words. Your friends, loved ones, and the other lives you may touch throughout your life will likely remember the goodwill you spread across your corner of the world than anything you ever said to them. Strive every day to be the person you want others to remember. If your neighbor, Joe, passed away, would ever hear someone say, "Joe told me the weather 20 years ago?" No, you may hear, "Joe fixed my car, so I would not be late for my son's graduation."

Deciding upon your goals is akin to planning your trip towards a Fabulous Life. If you clearly define your path from fair to fabulous, you will plot your course, accordingly, and every place your journey will take you. Think about your last vacation. Let's say, for example, you headed across the country. You surely plotted highways, sightseeing locations, and rest stops along the way. Planning ahead make for a smoother trip to paradise, right? Defining your goals allows you to pre-determine various aspects of your persona, your strengths and ways you can improve to prepare you for your fabulous future.

Now, you've heard the saying that you are what you eat? We are also the products of our thoughts. Mike Dooley, as another source of inspiration, creator of *Notes from the Universe* (http://www.tut.com) lives by the mantra that "thoughts become things... choose the good ones." His philosophy holds true for everyone. Once you set clear goals for yourself, define them, write them and commit them to memory, these aspirations have the ability to nag us into completing them, because our mind becomes accustomed to making our dreams a reality. The hardest part of all, though not all that difficult if you think about it, is taking that long, hard look inside us to determine what you want to accomplish. Realize that this transformation does not happen overnight, nor does the journey to a fabulous life, but neither did your cross country vacation.

Lastly, it is a sad reality that sometimes, people can be cruel. Despite your best laid plans in life, not everyone you meet will see you as fabulous, even if you accomplish the goal of seeing yourself in a brighter light. Remember that your path in life does not need to meet everyone else's. There will be plenty of people along your path to happiness to keep you company. Don't expend too much energy on those that aren't on your trail. By changing the way you see and speak to yourself as well as focusing on all the positives that are present in your life, your optimism will lift your spirits should the journey become rocky. Self-confidence is your beacon; self-doubt, just another of life's dreaded potholes!

You can definitely curb your self-doubt and inspire your self-confidence and be that beacon.

Chapter Three:

Controlling Worry

"There is only one way to happiness, and that is to cease worrying about things that are beyond the power of our will."

-Epictetus-

Have you ever had a dream where you woke up and were all sweaty or stressed out about something and then realized that it wasn't real? It sure felt real, didn't it? This is a simple illustration of the fact that stress or worry can be self-inflicted. Unless you are currently being chased by a murderer or are in some other life threatening event, there is nothing to worry about. But you can wake up sweating with a high heart rate just like it was happening, it is not.

But, Wayne you don't understand. My bills are all late. My kids are getting in trouble all the time. And, I'm about to get fired from work. I have a LOT to worry about!

No, you don't. You have issues to deal with, yes. But whether you have thoughts of worry or don't doesn't make a difference to whether you pay your bills, your kids get out of trouble, or you get fired. Those things are dependent on your actions not worrying about them. Worry is controllable because it is always "Self-Imposed". You can control your thoughts.

Are you naturally a "worrier?" Ask yourself, "What is my default personality?" What I mean by default is when someone happens what emotion do you display most often? Do family and friends call you positive/negative/helpful? Are you a leader or a follower; are you outgoing or quiet? Everyone has a unique default personality. My father always taught me that anyone can be nice or can be positive when the money is flowing and everyone is healthy. But who do you become when adversity strikes? We all default one way or the other. Is your default that the glass half full or half empty? Do you see what is good and right in most things you encounter or do you find yourself seeing mostly what is wrong or bad about that circumstance or person? This is when you must get honest with yourself if you want to improve. A battery has only two ends one end is the positive (+) and one end is the negative (-), you are one or the other... black and white.

Write your thoughts and feelings about your unique default personality here:

_____

_____

_____

_____

_____

_____

You can change your default personality. It is not permanent, just an old habit. It all starts with our thoughts and then our words. For example if you lean towards the glass being half empty, you can become one that leans towards the glass being half full. But it is a conscious decision, it takes hard work and we make the choice daily just like when we step into the closet and decide how to dress. You will need to work on it and practice as bad habits can be replaced with good habits. Like it takes exercise to strengthen a heart, it takes work to improve your mind.

So then from what you have written above, what is your default personality and how would you like to change it? Take a 3" x 5" card and write down who you would like to be, but do so with the frame of reference of defining your new default personality. Tape it to your bathroom mirror or in your closet where you dress or on the visor in your car. Remind yourself who you wish to become and see it as often as possible. Many times you will see on TV that a college or MLB player has something hand written inside the brim of their caps. This way every time they put on their cap it becomes a quick and simple positive reminder of who they are daily. We all need reminders that's why I am such a fan of Twitter as every day you can get access to as many excellent quotes about life as possible, kind of like positive brain food.

What do you do every day to set your personal tone? Do you pray; do you meditate? It is not going to happen on its own and if so may not be what you need to reach your goals.

What thoughts do you plant daily?

We all have an angel of self-confidence on one shoulder and a demon of self-doubt on the opposite shoulder. Which one is larger or more dominant? Every time I ask people this they look like a deer in the headlights, fearful of giving the wrong answer. The only correct answer is whichever one you feed the most. If you are a person that has a default towards what is wrong you will find exactly that, and if you are a person that has a default personality which always finds the silver lining in every dark cloud you too will find precisely the same result. Negative people often refer to themselves as realists and say this is foolish and positive people say yep you are absolutely correct. So, to change your default personality when it comes to worry, you need to tell yourself different things when worry starts. Which shoulder are you feeding daily?

I have told our sons to control what they can control and don't worry about the rest. There are so many things in this world that we simply cannot control and yet we get stressed out about so many of them. This is a complete waste of energy! Focus on what you can control and your daily point of reference or frame of mind about everything that happens to you is totally in your control. Each of us has a limited amount of mental fuel each day and we must spend it wisely but only on things that will improve our lives. If you will apply what we discuss in detail and do so for a minimum of 90 consecutive days, virtually everything in your life will improve. Because the change required to life improvement starts internally not externally.

"If you don't like something change it. If you can't change it, change your attitude."

-Maya Angelou-

In Proverbs 23:7 it clearly states "As a man thinketh in his heart so is he."

If 2013 years ago they knew that thoughts can transform our reality, why are so many people negative? Both of these quotes are dead on accurate and very powerful. How can you use them to help take your life from fair to fabulous and it only takes 15 minutes of focus daily?

Negative Self-Talk

Self-talks are those little conversations you have in your head that either support or undermine what you are trying to accomplish. These seemingly simple thoughts either take you closer or farther away from whom you want to be or accomplish. Yet few know how to control their thoughts. So how do you stop negative or "stinking" thinking? Remember our example about an acre of earth? If you till it, fertilize it, and give it some sunshine, what will grow on that acre of virgin soil? The answer is just like your mind, "Whatever you choose to plant" is what will grow. If you plant negative thoughts and emotions that is what you will get and if you plant positive thoughts and emotions those are the results that will grow. It is not easy; it takes work, like a diet, like working out in the gym, like running or riding a bike to keep your weight in a healthy range. You must commit to what you plant every day and do so with immense Gratitude.

So how do you master or control your negative thoughts? Once again the answer is to plant good thoughts. "How do you plant good thoughts?" Some may ask. Try starting a gratitude journal or even a 30-Day Gratitude Challenge or look up gratitude on Google. We all worry about many things - most of which never come true - and it is human nature to worry about your health, your job, your kids, and of course money and paying bills. The gratitude challenge will help you focus and realize all you have to be thankful for in your life. It helps us refocus; instead of on what we do not have, on what we do have and to be thankful or grateful for those treasures.

What do you take for granted? For example when someone loses their health, the first thing they might say is, "I should have taken better care of myself." It is sad that some do not appreciate all they have until it is gone and then often it is too late to get it back in their lives. Some unfortunately carry it to an extreme and the only things that come out of their most are pessimistic and worry filled thoughts.

Look up multiple Bible quotes on worry. You must have faith, not worry. Once again the only way to stop worry or negative thoughts is to consciously replace them with more positive thoughts. I know this is not easy, as it has taken years for you to allow these thoughts in your mind. Think of it like this: as some people have gotten out of shape and overweight, to change that they must change their habits; they must eat right and exercise. It took years to become out of shape; it will take some time to change.

Your mental mindset (default personality) is no different as it took years of improper thinking flowing around in your head to become half empty, it will take work and time to go back to being half full. The best part is—unlike shedding weight—you can shed these bad thoughts immediately with enough practice and positive reinforcement. You can start today, you can start right now, and you get to choose: just like when you choose what to wear or when you choose to read this book. You Are In Control, and it starts with the thoughts your "choose" to plant in your mind. Be strong make a commitment to change your life.

"If I have the belief that I can do it, I shall surely acquire the capacity to do it even if I may not have it at the beginning."

-Gandhi-

Worry is a self-imposed emotion and being a loving and devoted parent with my wife of our two sons—I can tell you that—we have both worried about them far too often when nothing bad happened at all that moment. You need to replace those thoughts with positive self-talk.

What are some things you can tell yourself when you start to worry?

1. _____

2. _____

3. _____

4. _____

5. _____

Here are some other ideas for controlling worry.

- Keep a worry diary of all your worrisome thoughts. But, instead of just writing them down, underneath each one, write down a reason that this is not something to worry about. For example, if you write, "I am worried I will get fired," then write "Instead of worrying I will go into work early."

- Set aside a time to worry. This may seem counterintuitive, but if you tell yourself, "I'll worry about that at 8:00 tomorrow morning," you can break the habit of worrying. By the time 8:00 am rolls around, you might not be worried about it anymore.

- Listen to the worry. Sometimes those nagging thoughts have something valuable to say. If, for example, you are worried that your spouse will leave you, then take a look at your marriage. Is it a rational fear? Are you having marriage problems? What is the worry trying to tell you?

"Faith is to believe what you do not see; the reward of this faith is to see what you believe."

-Saint Augustine-

Anyone reading this book needs to watch the YouTube videos for Adam Bender, the boy with one leg that plays all sports, or Anthony Robles the young man that won the ESPY by going undefeated his senior season at Arizona as a national championship wrestler to know this fact. Adversity hit each of them much more than it has 99% of those reading this book and yet they not only survived, but they found a way to thrive in the midst of the most negative situations and circumstances you could imagine. They've survived much more than you and I have ever faced and yet they find things in their lives to be thankful for daily. How did they accomplish so much against all odds? They made a decision to become in charge of their thoughts. In the movie *Rudy* everyone including his own father tells him what he cannot do, but he and his best friend believe he can do it, go watch this movie and then apply that technique to something in your life.

The book *Good to Great* is but another stellar example of mental mindset management. This book teaches all of us that Good is the enemy of Great as when you are okay with just being good you will never pay the price to be great. Unless you are unsatisfied with something that is just good, fair, or OK you will most likely never feel great or fabulous. It is hard to raise your level of expectations and as I have told our sons anything that is easy generally isn't worth a darn thing. Adversity and difficulty can be our greatest teachers or also can be what brings you down by denying the opportunity for greatness. What do you currently have in your life that is just good, what are you willing to exchange in order for that to be great? Tim Tebow once said "hard work will outperform talent when talent doesn't work hard." Many times it is not circumstance that determines one's place in life but just good old fashioned hard work. Good to Great can have so many applications in your personal and professional life.

Just as I did with you in the beginning of this book, ask the people you see today, "How are you today?" Then record their answers. When they ask how you are doing, pick an adjective that inspires you such as "fabulous," "wonderful," "remarkable," "blessed," "grateful." Then watch their faces when you answer them. Your daily default mindset starts with the words that you plant in your mind and then the words that you choose will come out of your mouth. Try it, commit to it, and when people ask you how you are, answer with that word.

Watching the News

I was driving to get breakfast today and for some odd reason turned on the radio to a morning news show. They were talking about a man that was hit by a train and had a severed arm and a woman's house that had burned down with her children in it and how she was in jailed charged for negligence. It was so depressing and I thought people are allowing this mental pollution to be planted in their brains to start the day, no wonder so many people default to what is wrong in this world opposed to focusing on what is right, good, and healthy. No one does this on purpose so think of it like going on a diet. Meaning when you are on a diet to lose weight you are very careful what you put into your body. Try the same exercise but with what you allow to be placed into your brain. Key word "allow" as we do get to choose what thoughts we embrace. Ironically the people listening to that broadcast could become very upset or even depressed today and never know why, not knowing they started their day with so much negative information being planted. Be aware and make a choice of what you listen too or read every day.

We cannot say the world is perfect or say there isn't bad news, we just get to choose what we focus on daily. This is why having an "Attitude of Gratitude" every day is crucial to a happier more rewarding life. Like you would monitor your food intake you must also monitor your informational intake, feed your brain with Zig Ziglar, Brian Tracy, Tony Robbins, Brian Cain, and of course watch the movie *The Secret*. Read and reread this book at least 15 minutes a day, do something on purpose to plant optimism in your life.

Like the mental side of hitting in college baseball, when at the plate should the hitter be thinking about the last time he struck out or should he be thinking *I am going to hit this next pitch somewhere really hard*? I know you're thinking you can't think yourself into hitting. Okay, maybe but you can TILT the odds in your favor. There is no question that a positive thought process helps and that the opposite hurts. So take say a 10% edge in your favor and then a -10% edge against you and look at the spread. If you think positively opposed to negatively, the overall spread could be as much as +20%, who doesn't want that edge/advantage/opportunity?

There are No Guarantees in life, in sports, in school, or in marriage, but you can tilt the odds in your favor. There is no question a person that has set written goals has an advantage at a more successful life. Just like a person that is more positive and optimistic than negative or pessimistic has a greater chance of success at everything. Not to mention the benefits of just feeling fabulous overall. You must believe you are in complete control of your daily thoughts.

Then why isn't everyone fabulous? Why are so many people walking around and when you say 'how are you,' they say 'fair' or just 'OK'? Because it takes work and it is easier to be negative. Because it is hard work to create the correct attitude and it is easy to run away from success. It is much harder to be positive, to stay positive, and to work on being positive. So if you want that six pack then you have to hit the weights if you want the rewards of hard work.

The same is true of being that person you want to be, the person you wrote down you want to be remembered as when you leave behind the job or this world. You have to hit the weight room and in this case, it is the mental weight room. By the way, this book is clearly a gymnasium for the brain because you are working hard right now, instead of wasting time. Don't get me wrong I love a break as much as anyone else, but only after working out mentally.

So we know the right mental mindset improves our odds or winning and of having longer lasting family relationships. We know that a fabulous attitude/mindset definitely increases the odds of success at work while earning more money to land a better job. It increases the chances of having more friends and a rich rewarding life. It also impacts your friends and family members but we have agreed it is not easy. If you know anyone that always finds fault with others, it is simple they are mentally weak and take the path of least resistance. You can make a difference, but this is not just about you as we can all make a difference in the lives that need us.

Then what are you waiting for? Let's get started changing some lives of those you love.

Chapter Three Summary

Worry can, and most of the time is, something we inflict upon ourselves. When we worry about financial burdens, problems that our children experience, or being fired from a job, those anxious moments solve nothing. Worry leads to stress, which can lead to a laundry list of health issues; only action has the ability to solve debt crises, discipline our children or push us to perform better at work. The best way to manage worry is to control your thoughts. Take the time to think about or ask others how you are viewed and then listen to the feedback, even if the feedback is simply listening to your own inner voice. Asking others for feedback is no different than checking the gauges in your car before you head off on vacation. You want to be sure the car is in tip-top shape for the trip; likewise, you want to be sure you are performing to the best of your ability when interacting with others throughout your day. Once you understand your default personality, you will be able to determine if you are in need of a personal "tune up." Just like an oil change and tire rotation for your vehicle before a trip, you must maintain your life to ensure that each day you live; you do so at your best performance.

Everyone has self-confidence and self-doubt. Many times—much too often—it becomes easier to focus on what we cannot control. Those unable to separate the things we can or cannot control, unfortunately, set themselves up for health issues that stress and worry can cause. According to WebMD, these complications of worry include heart disease, asthma, obesity, diabetes, headaches, depression and anxiety, gastrointestinal disorders, an increased risk for Alzheimer's disease, accelerated aging and premature death. Learning how to control your thoughts and to stop yourself when negativity calls is key to reaching your destination of Fabulous. Remember that whatever we plant is what we will reap, so instill positivity in your mind, each and every day. Michele Rosenthal, a trauma coach, Post Traumatic Stress Disorder survivor, and author of BEFORE THE WORLD INTRUDED, recently discussed in an e-newsletter how individuals under traumatic circumstances or life difficulties often feel disconnected to their inner sources of wisdom and worth. The best way to reconnect with yourself to allow you the opportunity to reach your goals is to follow your intuition because your inner voice not only knows you better than you may know yourself, but it also knows exactly when and how you need something at any given time.

Having healthy self-esteem has been scientifically proven to increase one's resilience. Positivity attracts positive people into our lives; negativity leaves you stuck in an abyss of difficult people and equally difficult situations. How you present yourself to others, but more importantly how the person staring back at you in the mirror sees you, sends clues to everyone you meet. To help you to become more aware of the positives in your life, consider using a gratitude journal, volunteering your time to those less fortunate, rely on faith with the knowledge that no difficult time lasts forever because the "road" of life winds and bends several times for everyone's lives. You can commit to freeing yourself from worry by creating a set time each day to do nothing but worry. Once you get the clutter removed from your mind, you will be better able to spend the rest of the day on something positive. While in your set time to worry, writing your worry and following it with a positive thought as to why the worry really is not as important as an action to fix the situation may be of assistance to you.

If you listen to your worry, you may be able to determine if the concern is valid or not. I recently met a young writer who shared with me a story that ties into this thought quite well. She spoke of how she was just 22 years old and decided, a little over a decade ago, to make her passion for writing a career choice. She joined an online writing critique site and at first, her reviews were favorable. Then, she received a few critical reviews, which devastated her and so frustrated her that she nearly quit writing. Of her critiques, some were favorable with pointers to assist her career; others were rude. She told me that her father noted her concern about the critics and said, "If you have critics, Jill, you must be doing something right or they would have nothing of worth to criticize." By framing the situation in a positive light, this young writer has continued to write, now has over a decade of experience, and is nationally published, whereas self-doubt and criticism had once led her to almost quit. From the day Jill realized that criticism was either a valid chance for growth or simply someone's opposing opinion, she framed her personal belief in herself and in her ability and solidified positivity, traits that keep her writing still today. This lesson is true for everyone in life, regardless of their career or life circumstance. Life has no guarantees and critics, like speed bumps and potholes in the road, are often inevitable, but how we respond when facing adversity will either serve as a setback or a "push forward," bringing us closer to the destination of living a Fabulous life! So, if you will, think of this: Leave the fair life to the critics, rid yourself of worry and self-doubt and get ready to thrive because when you find your own personal levels of self-confidence you're destined for greatness!

Chapter Four:

Planting Positive Seeds

**"The thing always happens that you really believe in;
and the belief in a thing is what makes it happen."**

-Frank Lloyd Wright-

One last time we repeat, if you had a barren one acre plot of land and then tilled that acre of earth you now have nothing in that dirt but very fertile soil, correct? If you leave that acre of earth barren what grows with the proper sunlight and water? The answer is weeds, those nasty plants the wind blows onto your land or are brought in by others from their shoes. (Like people that complain to you and dump their worries and leave) Then if you planted something in that fertile earth and gave it plenty of water and precisely the right amount sunshine, what would grow? The answer should be pretty easy: whatever you plant is what will grow. If you planted carrot seeds you will get carrots, not tomatoes. If you plant negatives they will grow but if you plant positive thoughts that is also what will grow. The best part is you choose "daily" what to plant each night when you go to sleep. One of life's blessing is tomorrow is a new day and that acre of earth will embrace whatever you plant just like your mind will do the same. So the exact same thing is true with your daily mindset. Whatever you plant is precisely what will grow.

Am I saying that you can dunk a ball like Kobe Bryant if you are only 5'5" with enough positive thoughts, or that you can hit a golf ball like Tiger Woods? No not at all. What I am saying is that even if you possessed the natural athletic talent of Kobe and Tiger, but you planted mental seeds of failure, you would never become as successful as they are in your life or chosen profession. One thing you can read is that talent is over rated, as talent alone does not make people succeed. What we know for sure is that true winners are mental giants and athletes like Kobe and Tiger work on positive mindset management frequently.

Whatever your favorite sport, list the attributes of your favorite stars on those teams. They may have speed, they may have athletic bodies, they many have physical strength, they may have many things we do not. But one thing they absolutely must have that you too must have is a strong mental mindset and that takes work.

My father was an unconscious competent at attitude mentoring as when you asked him how he was doing he would always say "Just South of Great" and his voice mail message always ended with "You Have an Awesome Day". He has never met a stranger and I've honestly never met anyone more universally loved than my dad. He is without question one of the most positive people I ever met and has blessed me with the foundation I need to not only raise my family and have the job I have but also to eventually write this book. He and I both believe there are so many things in this world you cannot control. You cannot control traffic, taxes, gas prices, but you have "total" control over your attitude each and every day. After reading this "What will you say when people ask how are you today?"

> **"We are what we repeatedly do. Excellence,**
> **therefore, is not an act but a habit."**
>
> **-Aristotle-**

As we have discussed, have you ever asked yourself, "What is the difference between the person I want to be and the person that other people see?" Are they close to the same or way far apart as if they are far apart you have the power to change that right now, today, as soon as you finish reading? How by simply making the choice to refuse to be less than fabulous? Would anyone say you are the most positive person they know at work, at home, in sports?

In my 30+ year career, I have worked for 3 great companies, two Fortune 500 companies and the most recent a world class branded single site sales center that could create over $150,000,000 in annual revenue. It is located in Hawaii and is the most fabulous property I have ever seen filled with great people and a product unmatched anywhere in their respective industry. As you can imagine I met some extremely successful people there and here is where this short story begins. As one of two of the most senior sales leaders at this site I was officed near a top performing sales manager that worked with an international speaking sales team. He had been there for many years and, loves his company, his brand, his sales team, his property, just a super high integrity guy in every way possible. I really enjoyed our conversations, especially about learning how each department sells the same product to two cultures so seemingly unique from different locations of the world.

Virtually every day we were among the first two in the office. It took some time to get to know him as once he was at work; the day was full steam ahead very quickly at a property this large. Once I got to know him better, I started a new part of our journey together. Every morning when he would come in, I would ask him 'how are you today'? Generally, his default answer was 'Fair', 'Fine', 'Good', Etc which of course was fine for him as he was busy working. Without question, he may be one of the most positive and optimistic people in those offices. If asked, I couldn't say enough great things about him and what he brings that sales team. So I felt it was time for us to have an initial discussion about resetting our mental mind set daily and how regardless of the stress or performance pressure from end of month budgets, our people would look to us to set the tone daily and that seemed to make sense to him.

Every morning after he gave me the 'Fair', 'Fine', 'Good', response I would walk over to his office and say "Excuse me, how are you today"? He would look up from the reports he was already deeply involved in from prior daily sales and say with a huge grin, "well I am just Wonderful, Fantastic, Fabulous", et cetera. It took some time and we'd even joked when he'd slip back to the old default response but he did—after some repetition—finally make an effort to reset his default mental mindset to Fabulous. On the few minor occasions he may have faltered, he then would quickly come to my office again sharing a huge smile and immediately correct himself. I loved catching him and he grew stronger while starting to catch himself, you can too.

I do not have access to his sales numbers so I cannot say this one example made him more sales revenue but what I can absolutely guarantee is he is enjoying the journey more. During my last few weeks there, we went to lunch and when I got in the car I said 'how are you today', and he couldn't say 'fabulous' fast enough! Once again with his priceless grin that would make even the most upset customer or employee smile. Discover what your mental mindset can do as our brain is the one muscle we need to train the most and many generally spend the least time working on improving as it should and can become your daily default experience!

Acres of Diamonds

Here is one of the most famous speeches ever given. It was given by a man named Russell Conwell and is called "Acres of Diamonds."

There's more to the speech, but what I'm including here is the relevant part of us in this chapter.

There once lived not far from the River Indus an ancient Persian by the name of Ali Hafed. He said that Ali Hafed owned a very large farm; that he had orchards, grain-fields, and gardens; that he had money at interest and was a wealthy and contented man. One day there visited that old Persian farmer one of those ancient Buddhist priests, one of the wise men of the East. He sat down by the fire and told the old farmer how this old world of ours was made.

He said that this world was once a mere bank of fog, and that the Almighty thrust His finger into this bank of fog, and began slowly to move His finger around, increasing the speed until at last He whirled this bank of fog into a solid ball of fire. Then it went rolling through the universe, burning its way through other banks of fog, and condensed the moisture without, until it fell in floods of rain upon its hot surface, and cooled the outward crust. Then the internal fires bursting outward through the crust threw up the mountains and hills, the valleys, the plains and prairies of this wonderful world of ours. If this internal molten mass came bursting out and cooled very quickly, it became granite; less quickly copper, less quickly silver, less quickly gold, and, after gold, diamonds were made. Said the old priest, "A diamond is a congealed drop of sunlight." Now that is literally scientifically true, that a diamond is an actual deposit of carbon from the sun.

The old priest told Ali Hafed that if he had one diamond the size of his thumb he could purchase the county, and if he had a mine of diamonds he could place his children upon thrones through the influence of their great wealth. Ali Hafed heard all about diamonds, how much they were worth, and went to his bed that night a poor man. He had not lost anything, but he was poor because he was discontented, and discontented because he feared he was poor. He said, "I want a mine of diamonds," and he lay awake all night. Early in the morning he sought out the priest. I know by experience that a priest is very cross when awakened early in the morning, and when he shook that old priest out of his dreams, Ali Hafed said to him:

"Will you tell me where I find diamonds?"

"Diamonds! What do you want with diamonds?"

"Why, I wish to be immensely rich."

"Well, then, go along and find them. That is all you have to do; go and find them, and then you have them."

"But I don't know where to go."

"Well, if you will find a river that runs through white sands, between high mountains, in those white sands you will always find diamonds."

"I don't believe there is any such river."

"Oh yes, there are plenty of them. All you have to do is to go and find them, and then you have them."

Said Ali Hafed, "I will go."

So he sold his farm, collected his money, left his family in charge of a neighbor, and away he went in search of diamonds. He began his search, very properly to my mind, at the Mountains of the Moon. Afterward he came around into Palestine, then wandered on into Europe, and at last when his money was all spent and he was in rags, wretchedness, and poverty, he stood on the shore of that bay at Barcelona, in Spain, when a great tidal wave came rolling in between the pillars of Hercules, and the poor, afflicted, suffering, dying man could not resist the awful temptation to cast himself into that incoming tide, and he sank beneath its foaming crest, never to rise in this life again.

Then after that old guide had told me that awfully sad story, he stopped the camel I was riding on and went back to fix the baggage that was coming off another camel, and I had an opportunity to muse over his story while he was gone. I remember saying to myself,

"Why did he reserve that story for his 'particular friends'?" There seemed to be no beginning, no middle, no end, nothing to it.

That was the first story I had ever heard told in my life, and would be the first one I ever read, in which the hero was killed in the first chapter. I had but one chapter of that story, and the hero was dead. When the guide came back and took up the halter of my camel, he went right ahead with the story, into the second chapter, just as though there had been no break.

The man who purchased Ali Hafed's farm one day led his camel into the garden to drink, and as that camel put its nose into the shallow water of that garden brook, Ali Hafed's successor noticed a curious flash of light from the white sands of the stream. He pulled out a black stone having an eye of light reflecting all the hues of the rainbow. He took the pebble into the house and put it on the mantel which covers the central fires, and forgot all about it.

A few days later this same old priest came in to visit Ali Hafed's successor, and the moment he opened that drawing-room door he saw that flash of light on the mantel, and he rushed up to it, and shouted:

"Here is a diamond! Has Ali Hafed returned?"

"Oh no, Ali Hafed has not returned, and that is not a diamond. That is nothing but a stone we found right out here in our own garden."

"But," said the priest, "I tell you I know a diamond when I see it. I know positively that is a diamond."

Then together they rushed out into that old garden and stirred up the white sands with their fingers, and lo! There came up other more beautiful and valuable gems then the first. "Thus," said the guide to me, "was discovered the diamond-mine of Golconda, the most magnificent diamond-mine in all the history of mankind, excelling the Kimberly itself. The Kohinoor, and the Orloff of the crown jewels of England and Russia, the largest on earth, came from that mine."

You see, the point of this story is that you already have everything you need to live a fabulous life. You have a mind that can plant seeds of positivity. You don't need to travel the world searching for it. It's already in your own backyard.

"Every time you subtract a negative from your life, you make immediate room for more positive results."

-- Author Unknown

Now it's time for an exercise. In the following space, write down some of the negative seeds you've been planting.

_____

_____

_____

_____

_____

"Positive thinking will let you do everything better than negative thinking will."

-Zig Ziglar-

Now, write down the positive ones you'll plant from today on.

_____

_____

_____

_____

_____

"If you do not change direction, you are going to end up where you are heading."

-Lao Tzu-

Changing direction starts with changing your thought process. So to change direction as the quote says above you need to know about NLP. There is a very detailed theory with the initials NLP that stands for Neuro Linguistic Programming. (Neuro for mind, linguistic for language, programming for behavior change) One more time another very accepted theory that states it starts with our mind something we totally control, then with our words. There are many books and online articles that support this concept in more detail. I reference this published theory because once again it fully supports all the concepts in this book in that everything in our lives today starts from how we think. Basically it says we have the ability to program ourselves with first what we say with our words and then with what we do with our actions. What are you doing today to program yourself using NLP? Meditation can be a form of NLP as the deepest of thinkers can help program out negative thoughts by replacing them with more positive thoughts.

An online definition of NLP is; "the basic premise of NLP is that the words we use reflect an inner subconscious perception. So if these words and perceptions are inaccurate, as long as we continue to use them, the underlying problem will persist. In other words, our attitudes are, in a sense, a self-fulfilling prophecy." As said in the computer world "garbage in garbage out" You need to train yourself how to reprogram your thoughts to those of gratitude and appreciation; you are in control. Now we even have more support: it starts with our thoughts.

We all know people that can find something wrong with anything and even those that are sort of hypochondriacs and think the worst of their health and everything about their lives. Again, if in the game of baseball, do you stand at the plate with self-talk that repeats 'I am going to smash this ball' or do you allow the boogie man in your head saying 'I hope I don't strike out'? It once again says that thoughts are things and though we can't guarantee it we can increase your odds of success with more positive thoughts opposed to thinking negatively. NLP teaches us many things and there are many online training programs to teach you how to plant more positive thoughts that can in fact lead to a happier healthier life. That we can and have the power to tilt the odds in our favor daily. That we can choose now to stop the negative thinking and replace it with love and gratitude. You can easily go online and find a great wealth of information about NLP techniques and those that have used them with great success. It is in a simple nutshell that the science of planting thoughts and that what you plant definitely influences the overall results of everything you do. Watch how professional athletes see their success first.

"He has achieved success who has lived well,
laughed often and loved much;
who has gained the respect of intelligent men and the love of little
children; who has filled his niche and accomplished
his task; who has left the
world better than he found it, whether
by an improved poppy, a perfect poem,
or a rescued soul; who has never lacked appreciation of earth's beauty or
failed to express it; who has always looked for the best in others and given
them the best he had; whose life was an inspiration;
whose memory a benediction."

-Bessie Stanley, 1905, commonly misattributed
to Ralph Waldo Emerson-

Now there's a vision statement to strive for daily. How would you like people to say that defines you and your life? That you left everywhere you went a better place. We can become that person just like we can have a Fabulous life. You have to believe we are in control every day. You must embrace the proven fact that everything we do and everything we are starts with our thoughts and that we get to make those choices every day. What is your vision of you today?

Do you believe you get to choose your attitude every single day? Do you believe that it is never what happens but how we choose to deal with what happens that will ultimately determine the outcome of almost every situation in our lives? What do you believe, what are your goals, what is the vision you have painted for your life? When we get into a car, we know where we are going. We get a map or a GPS and off we go to a precise destination. When you got up today where are you going in your life? What road map do you use; what is your GPS? College students know precisely what classes to take to get the degree of their choice and then they take those classes. How can you get somewhere if you do not know precisely here you are going? Do you have written goals? When are you going to sit down and start with 3, then 5, then 7? I have written 15-18 goals every year the last 20 plus years, surprisingly one of them was to write a book and this one has taken longer to do than any other, more difficult and more rewarding.

"Happiness is when what you think, what you say, and what you do are in harmony."

-Mohandas Gandhi-

Is there any more powerful a one line quote ever spoken? How can we merge those three together, Thoughts-Words-Actions? It is possible but once again starts with our thoughts every day. When your thoughts, then your words, and finally your actions are all on the same page, something magical happens.

Have you ever seen the movie with Robin Williams where Julia Roberts plays Tinker Bell? She asks him, "What are your happy thoughts?" Without them, he cannot remember he is actually Peter Pan? Yes it is make-believe and a cool Disney movie but the premise is very sound and closely matches the quote above. Happiness is when what you think, what you say, and what you do are in harmony. What are your happy thoughts; what are you grateful for in your life right this minute? We are so blessed. Do you have happy fabulous thoughts, you do get a choice? Focus on what you are grateful for as often as possible. This will make a difference.

Do you have a vision quest or even a personal vision statement that you read frequently? Some I know do vision boards to keep them focused and on track. What are the boundaries in your life? Meaning what will you tolerate and what will you not? What are your non-negotiables? There are so many things out there to help you help yourself. Where do you see yourself in five years and/or where do you want to be in five years? What is your vision as for example in the Bible it says those without vision will perish. What is the difference between the person you want to be and the person others see? You must believe you are in control and happiness is not the destination but your personal journey.

A vision board is an elaborate way to have written goals but with pictures. You develop one for yourself and then place it somewhere that you can see it every day. The purpose is simple and that is when you see every day what you want, you will gravitate towards those goals. I remember someone once said to me, 'Wayne, if you make me a manager I will become more responsible and more positive every day.' I said to him, 'become more positive and responsible and your peers will follow you. Then we will have no choice but to make you a manager.'

Life is like an empty box as you can never take out more than you put in and the secret is you have to make all your deposits in advance. You cannot say give me money and I will be fabulous or give me a new car and I will have a great attitude. You have to believe that you can be fabulous; you have to plant great thoughts every day, regardless of how tough the prior day may have been. You have to forgive those that have hurt you and move on, you have to love unconditionally and be grateful about something every single day. You have to make every day better than when you found it and pay it forward without expecting anything in return. You must believe that all of the above starts with the choice you get every day to select your mindset. For example, no one can hurt you without your permission; do you react or do you respond?

Do you know who can actually be responsible for sabotaging your success? You know this person very well, but sometimes most people do not realize who is holding you back. Are you ready to reveal who the culprit is? Well, believe it or not it can actually be you. Let me explain why I say this and as when I say that "you're sabotaging yourself" I mean that some of your thoughts you may not even be aware of are unintentionally undermining your success. These thoughts can be called "limiting beliefs," and some say we form them at a very young age, and everyone, yes everyone, has them, so you're not alone. Most of us are completely unaware that we have limiting beliefs. We must replace them with profound thoughts of personal belief.

**It is what a person thinks of himself that
really determines his fate.**

-Henry David Thoreau-

If you believe the quote above then what will you do to immediately improve the quality of your thoughts? We know that they have a lasting impact and it is more than worth the effort. But like everything else worth having this will not come to you not come easy without hard work

Chapter Four Summary

Planting positive seeds in every aspect of our lives from our thinking to our actions serves to spread happiness throughout our corner of the world. Maybe you have noticed, as most have, that being around a negative person can make even the most positive spirit feel a little blue, even if only in feeling sorry for their negativity. One's frame of mind and the beliefs you place into the world have the ability to affect not only you personally, but everyone we come to meet.

Imagine that you love your career and perform your tasks very well, you have a mutual respect and understanding among your dedicated and punctual co-workers, and you have framed your mind to realize you give your best and your heart or soul to the work you do every day. You have grown so much that your positivity makes your office an inviting place and your co-workers view working with you as a blessing. That's the way to live your life, right? Yes. Now, imagine that your boss is someone without positive energy. Let's us she is someone that fails to accept any responsibility for her own decisions, blames others for her mistakes, constantly causes chaos by questioning your decisions or your work and may even go so far as to question why you bother showing up to work at all. The more you try to go out of your way to please her, the harder you try to do an even more exemplary job, the more she berates and fails to see that her issue is not with you, but a negativity within herself. If you have framed your mind to know that you do the best job you possibly can, you might be able to deflect your negative boss's blows to your psyche, but in remembering that you are only responsible for yourself, you may also decide the environment is not for you and thus, you choose to walk away and avoid the drama. This is a good example of how negative seeds can impact everyone near chaotic spouts.

For a brief moment, think again about a garden. What happens to a healthy garden when weeds invade? The weeds, if not pruned, take over, choking and thus damaging your once healthy plants. A life lesson that many children learn at a young age is to be a leader and not a follower. Leaders remain resilient and positive; followers tend to go with the flow and can get caught up in others' issues. Since you can choose your attitude daily, would you rather be the positive employee that inspires the office or the negative boss that makes life tougher for all? I'll bet I know which one you'll choose. Living a fabulous life allows you to enjoy life more and the more you enjoy your life, the more others will pick up on your energy and thrive.

If you find yourself lacking a little in the positivity department, that's okay for this point in time. If one thing is for certain, everyone's brains need training, even those belonging to the most inspiring people in the world. You can train your brain to become more positive because you have all the tools you need to achieve this. I am reminded of Lou Gehrig's "Luckiest Man" farewell speech of July 4, 1939 and college basketball coach, Jim Valvano's ESPY speech of March 4, 1993. Both sports figures faced illnesses that would later take their lives. Gehrig said, in speaking of his "bad break," still saw himself as "the luckiest man on the face of this earth" because he appreciated the blessings that his baseball career bestowed upon him. He accepted that his life "may have had a tough break" but that he had "an awful lot to live for." Valvano stated that cancer could take away all of his abilities, but it could not touch his mind, it could not touch his heart, and it could not touch his soul. Despite challenges, these two men are shining examples for how happiness, even in times of hardship, exists when what you think, say and do are in harmony.

If you struggle with seeing your goals and how to make them work for you, consider creating a vision board with pictures to assist you with gravitating towards what you want to achieve in your life. Vision boards are simple to make and there are subtle tricks to making an inspiring one. For some, making an anti-vision board of what you don't want in life can be inspiring. For most, feeling your way through creating your vision board allows you to take stock in what really is the most important to you. For example, taking too much time to create your board may make you realize that you are prone to putting everything and everyone else in life ahead of your own needs. You must create a vision of you to memorize, internalize, and personalize.

Cliché as it may be, life truly is what we make of it. We reap what we sow and we can become our own worst enemy when it comes to success, if we gravitate towards negativity or limiting beliefs, whether our own or the limiting beliefs of others. How can outside forces sabotage our thinking and lead to the creation of our own limiting beliefs? I'll share an example:

In a rural Midwestern community of 6,000 residents back in 1990, there was a 19 year old man that came from a family that was labeled trouble by the small town gossipers. Despite being judged because of his family and growing up believing that nothing good ever comes to those from small towns, the young man had one major asset going for him: a 95-mph fastball. Soon thereafter, the pitching Phenom and his friend traveled across the Midwest with the hope of displaying the talent before Major League Baseball scouts. The scouts were impressed, but the young man's grades in high school were less than par and a four-year college was not an option. A year passed. Still committed to believing in the young man, his friend – who had since moved to Texas – offered to find the ballplayer a job, help him get into junior college and onto a baseball team the college launched that year. The young man left his parents' home in the Midwest, moved to Texas and enrolled at the junior college, found a job, and everything seemed to be going great. Then, the limiting beliefs of his family, the comments of how he would never amount to anything, how he didn't deserve anything, etc. trickled through phone calls with his family and friends back home. The young man dropped out of school, quit his job, and moved back to his rural small town. Four players from that junior college baseball team made it to the Majors, but because the young man allowed the limiting beliefs instilled upon him to override his potential, he was not the fifth. Would he have made the Majors? Would he have been the fifth player from the team to make it? It's impossible to say, but you often hear that if you don't play the lottery, you are assured you will not win the jackpot. The same philosophy holds true in this scenario. Because the young man allowed limiting beliefs that told him that he did not deserve the best to change his course, he still lives with regret, always wondering and never knowing what might have been.

This is a prime example of how limiting thoughts and the negativity of others can impact those that have not learned how to live a fabulous life. If you follow the exercises in this book, you will find smoother sailing on your road to Fabulous. Your dreams are in sight. Are you ready to reach them? That will only happen with extra effort.

Everything in this life has a price so precisely what are you willing to exchange to get the result that you desire? We know there is no free lunch, find your own inspiration. A great source of inspiring stories can be found on you tube, like Richie Parker an engineering graduate from Clemson University. No big deal right, except he was born with no hands but still went to college got a degree in engineering and designs cars with a computer using his feet. He is living proof that anyone can do anything, a very inspirational positive personal accomplishment.

Chapter Five:

Overcoming Adversity

"Faith is to believe what you do not see; the reward of this faith is to see what you believe."

-Saint Augustine-

You must believe you can make a change in your life regardless of current circumstances. Everyone has adversity. You do, I do, and everyone does. So, what is the difference between a person who experiences terrible adversity and rises above it and one who uses it as an excuse for failure? The answer is a mindset and thoughts of persistence! Let's look at several examples of some famous people you might recognize who had adversities that you might not know about.

- Basketball star Michael Jordan didn't make his high school basketball team. He was later named the greatest athlete of the 20th Century by ESPN.

- Sex symbol Marilyn Monroe was dropped in 1947 by 20th Century Fox after one year under contract because production chief Darryl Zanuck thought she was unattractive.

- Dr. Seuss's first book was rejected by 27 publishers and Seuss considered burning the manuscript. The eventual publisher sold six million copies.

- Singer and actress Barbra Streisand's Broadway debut opened and closed on the same night.

- Actor Tom Cruise was rejected for a role on the TV show *FAME* because he wasn't "pretty enough."

- Walt Disney's first cartoon production company went bankrupt.

- George Lucas' first film flopped in 1971 prompting every major studio to turn down his next movie, *AMERICAN GRAFFITI.*

- Orville Wright was expelled from the 6th grade for mischievous behavior.

- Christopher Columbus miscalculated the size of the globe and the width of the Atlantic Ocean and wound up discovering the island of San Salvador in the Bahamas (which he believed to be an island of the Indies), Cuba (which he thought be a part of China), and the Dominican Republic (which he also mistook as part of the Far East).

- Sylvester Stallone was thrown out of 14 schools in 11 years. His professors at the University of Miami discouraged him from a career in acting. Stallone was also rejected for roles in the movies, *DOG DAY AFTERNOON, SERPICO*, and *THE GODFATHER.* His screenplay for ROCKY was also rejected by all but one company, who insisted that if they bought it, he would not act in it.

- Billy Joel, embarrassed by his first album, *COLD SPRING HARBOR*, spent 6 months playing bar piano in the lounge of the Executive Room in Los Angeles under the pseudonym Bill Martin.

- Elvis Presley's music teacher at L. C. Humes High School in Memphis gave him a C and told him he couldn't sing.

- Jay Leno failed an employment test at Woolworth's.

- Billy Crystal was cut from the cast of Saturday Night Live before the show ever premiered.

- Barbara Walters was told to "stay out of television" in 1957 by a prominent producer.

- Clint Eastwood was fired by Universal studios after his first two movies for talking too slowly.

- Lucille Ball was told that she had no talent and should go home from Murray Anderson's drama school. Failing to get into any Broadway chorus lines, she worked as a waitress and soda jerk.

- Van Halen's first demo tape was rejected by every major record label.

- John F. Kennedy lost the election to be President of his freshman class at Harvard. He failed to win a post on the student council as a sophomore and dropped out of Stanford Business School.

- Thomas Edison was fired from his job working in a telegraph office after one of his experiments exploded.

- Dustin Hoffman, after failing to work as an actor in New York, worked as janitor and an attendant in a mental ward.

- Benjamin Franklin attended school for only two years.

- Katie Couric was banned from reading news reports on the air by the president of CNN because of her irritating, high-pitched, squeaky voice.

- Mick Jagger was deemed "unsuitable" by the BBC to sing on the radio in 1962

- Steven Spielberg's mediocre grades prevented him from getting accepted to UCLA film school.

- John Grisham's first novel was rejected by 16 agents and a dozen publishers. He later wrote *THE PELICAN BRIEF, THE CLIENT* and *THE FIRM*, which were all best sellers and were made into movies.

- During the first year, Coca-Cola only sold 400 Cokes.

- During his first three years in the automobile business, Henry Ford went bankrupt twice.

- R. H. Macy failed seven times before his store in New York caught on.

- Thomas Edison was thrown out of school in the early grades when the teachers decided he could not do the work.

- Bob Dylan was booed off the stage at his high school talent show.

- Thomas Edison tried more than 2, 000 experiments before he was able to get his light bulb to work.

- General Douglas MacArthur was denied admission to West Point twice.

- Academy Award-winning writer, producer and director Woody Allen failed motion picture production at New York University and City College of New York. He also flunked English at NYU.

- Albert Einstein didn't start speaking until he was 9 years old.

- Claude Monet had horrible cataracts. Fortunately he still became one of the world's greatest painters.

- Ludwig von Beethoven was deaf when he wrote some of his best music. Most people wouldn't think a deaf person could succeed in music.

- Rudyard Kipling submitted a story to a California newspaper in 1888. The editor replied, "I'm sorry Mr. Kipling, you just don't know how to use the English language." He later won the 1907 Nobel Prize for Literature.

- Randy Travis was rejected by every major record label twice.

- Babe Ruth holds the major league record for having struck out the most times in a career.

- Walter Payton never made it to a Division I school to play College football. He later became the NFL's career rushing yardage leader.

- Jerry Rice never made it to a Division I school to play College football. He later became the NFL's career leader in several receiving categories.

- In his first 20 years of business, Tom Monaghan went broke twice, lost control of his pizza company, and was sued for trademark violations. Later on that pizza company went on to become Domino's pizza.

- Luciano Pavarotti could not read music. He went on to become one of the leading Tenors in the world and still has trouble reading music!

**"True forgiveness is when you can say,
"Thank you for that experience."**

-Oprah Winfrey-

Basically, the bottom line is this. Everyone who has achieved fabulous success had something they needed to overcome. The difference between the ones who overcame adversity and those who do not is their mindset or in some cases their willpower. It is true if you want something bad enough you can get it as long as you believe you deserve it and you are willing to move heaven and earth to get it. If you think you can... you can, if you think you can't... you're right.

This premise has not changed throughout this e-book and is a foundation of my life. The older I get the more I have cut negative people out of my circle of trust. We have raised our boys by saying, "Show me your friends and I will show you your future." Why do you allow people around you to be negative? Do you allow yourself to say, feel, or think negatively and if so how do you stop those thoughts? Once again by stopping right then and right there to plant good thoughts, people you love, trips you have taken, gifts you have given or received that bring a smile to your face. Review your life in your mind's eye by thinking of what you love and adore about your spouse/kids/relatives, do not focus on what is wrong but what is right. It does work but it also takes practice and commitment and discipline to make it a habit, a good habit...

**"The difference between a successful person
and others is not a lack of strength, not a lack
of knowledge, but rather a lack of will."**

-Vince Lombardi-

If you expect good things in your life you have to have a good attitude first. It's easy to have a great attitude when everything is perfect, but show me someone with a great attitude in the midst of adversity and that is a person destined for success. Do you put more into your job than you take out? Do you put more into your relationships and do so without expecting anything in return? You need to think about living by the 100%/0% principle and that means giving 100% up front and expecting 0% in return. It sounds tough but it works. Trying reading Matthew 5:41.

What are the challenges you have or are facing?

_____

_____

_____

_____

_____

_____

How can this challenge actually become a blessing?

_____

_____

_____

_____

_____

In Chapter 5 of Brian Tracy's book *No Excuses: The Power of Self-Discipline*, he talks about what he calls "your biggest investment" in life.

He compares it to a muscle.

If you exercise it regularly, it will increase in strength over the years.

If you choose to ignore it, it will become weaker and decline over time.

Most people take it for granted, he says flatly. They even fail to realize that it's the biggest ongoing investment they make in their lives. It's the biggest investment you can ever make! Do you have the self-discipline to pick up this book for 15 minutes a day for the next 30 days?

**"Success consists of going from failure to
failure without loss of enthusiasm."**

~Winston Churchill

Here is a quick inspiring story about my sister who had a great invention to share. She flew all the way to California to make a presentation to the people at Shark Tank. Upon arrival she saw that some were camping out all night to save their place in line, so off she went to get a tent and chair to save her 41st place in line out of 500 they would see the next day. All night long she practiced her presentation until the next morning came and it was her turn to impress the panel. She was ready to go and as excited and enthusiastic as she had even been only to present her invention to a person with a stone face that pushed her to do so in a modest time frame. She left and was devastated as he clearly didn't get what she had to present as a guy and she was showing off her new invention that every woman in America would love to have in her bedroom. Dejected she went out and sat by the hotel pool and another woman came up to her and they basically shared the same experience. She had spent all this money to fly from Virginia plus a car, plus a room, plus expenses and it felt like a waste of time.

So what did she do, did she sit there and commiserate and wallow in her own pity and now even with someone else's negative experience to make her feel better? No, she did not; instead she tried a different technique for replacing her negative feelings and thoughts. Watch this as anyone can do this technique. She sat down and wrote herself a letter and in this letter she spoke about getting up again. That all successful people have adversity, that her idea was a great one and that she should try and try and try again until successful. She wrote many positive affirmations to herself about everything you could imagine to help make her feel better about this experience and to inspire her to continue the journey no matter how difficult. So what did she do? Simple. She replaced all those negative thoughts and negative emotions. She tilled the acre of earth in her brain of the weeds, and replaced everything destructive with positive thought and feelings and now has an entirely different viewpoint of the exact same situation. Now she is more fired up than prior to her presentation to prove her idea is a multi-million dollar winner. Not to mention she feels better and now has reinvigorated her personal drive to get up and get after it again. To never give up on her dreams until she reaches that plateau. I was so impressed and am so proud of her that she inspired me to include this in this book so you too could share her brilliant idea.

In summary, the only way to get rid of negative thoughts it to throw out that trash and replace those thoughts with positive thoughts. Write yourself a letter and place it somewhere you can see it every day. Include a goal, a promotion, any vision you want to achieve and read it daily. You can easily do this with an investment of only fifteen minutes daily.

How badly do you want to make a change in your life? What are you willing to exchange to get the things you do want, to become the father/mother you want for your children? Do you desire to become a better coach in sports or in life? Do you desire to become a better leader or a better husband/wife to your spouse? You will never have a six pack without hitting the gym. Success at every level is only obtained by paying in advance. You can start today, right now.

Chapter Five Summary

You must believe you can change regardless of any adversity you may face. How we respond to life's adversity shapes our character and defines the direction our lives will take. Everyone that has found any realm of success has had to overcome something in life, whether rejection, personal challenges, or criticism, among others. This is why living life with a positive, non-judgmental mindset is so important. No one is immune to periods of personal trials. Just because someone may not choose to place their struggles on a billboard for everyone to see does not mean that trouble does not exist. A prime example of this would be someone struggling with an autoimmune disease. Many times, autoimmune conditions have symptoms that are internal, not physical, and sufferers look fine, but struggle daily. Unless you have a wealth of knowledge about autoimmune disease, you may not understand what the person is going through, but listening or offering support shapes your character and ensures you do not offend or add to another's burden.

In each life, there have been times when it seemed like a Midas touch existed and everything fell perfectly into place. Then, there are the times when nothing ever seemed to go right. It is how you respond to those times of adversity that mold the foundation of your character. If you choose to focus on the positives in life, as opposed to the negatives; if you give your all at every turn and expect nothing in return, you'll live a life of favor and in turn…. Fabulous. Think about the preemie no one expected to live that grew to live a life of helping others, so grateful for the gift of life or the survivor of abuse that uses her newfound safety to raise awareness and assist others to escape their own adverse situations. These two examples shine light on all that can be when the power of positive thinking is displayed front and center.

Speaking positive affirmations to yourself on a daily basis will help to keep your spirit grounded through those times of adversity and moments when your transformation from Fair to Fabulous seems to be moving as slowly as traffic on the interstate, sabotaging your pace to get to your destination. Remember, you possess a great deal of self-worth and have many personal gifts that you can and do bestow upon others, each and every day. While some see adversity as a negative factor in our lives, life's difficulties can fuel a fire within the soul that dares the mind and heart of those brave enough to rise to adversity's occasion and ride the wave to the end. This, in turn, can make the hardest of adversity seem like a blessing.

In September 2008, Hurricane Ike hit the Gulf Coast of Texas, causing a great deal of damage and incredible loss. For one family, the storm hit just a little over two-and-a-half months after the loss of the family's dear loved one and a couple of months before layoff rumors began, which would have left this family more devastated than the losses already incurred. When the family arrived home from their evacuation point, they returned to six feet of debris in their living room after their home's chimney fell through the roof, leaving an 18x24' hole between the home's two skylights. Neighbors flocked to the family's side to assist them and paused in amazement when the daughter looked through the hole in the roof to the blue sky beaming between the two skylights. It was then the daughter said, "Wow... a third skylight." No one could believe she was making jokes about such a difficult situation, but she framed the struggle to see the positives that remained. The sun still rose, the sky was clear, and while the house was damaged, it was more than others were left, and the family had their lives. A few months later, *Chicken Soup for the Soul* accepted the daughter's story of the amazing "third skylight" and others were inspired by her decision to turn a negative into a positive.

Can you imagine how different the world would be had Christopher Columbus not made his miscalculation, had Elvis Presley given up on his singing, and had Henry Ford decided two bankruptcies were proof enough that the automobile was a failure, to name a few of our examples? Can you imagine how different the world would be if your dreams were actually impossible? I can't. Your hopes, goals, and dreams are within your reach. All you have to do is go for them and vow fifteen minutes each day to bring them a little closer to the Fabulous life within your reach. A long time quote that sounds simple but has great meaning is, "If you think you can you can, if you think you can't you're right."

We all have times and situations in our life that can turn out to be negative or positive, what you need to believe if that you have the power to influence the final outcome. We spoke earlier about imposing your will, all that really means is that your belief that something will turn out positive is stronger than someone else's belief that it will turn out negative. Nothing good has ever occurred in your life that started out from negative thoughts, so tilt the odds on your favor.

Part Two

Fifteen Minutes to Fabulous

Now that we know what's been holding you back and you understand the ideas, it is time to get practical. In this part of the book, we'll address the three core areas of life and how you can make them fabulous in just fifteen minutes a day.

The reason this book is titled *Fair to Fabulous in Fifteen Minutes* is because we have developed a series of exercises and techniques that you can do in fifteen minute increments that will help you transform your life. It really doesn't take all that much time. You don't have to spend hours meditating and working out and writing in an affirmation journal to improve your life. It's far simpler than that. It's about implementing some minor but daily changes into your life and the way you think and interact with people. You really can go from fair to fabulous in fifteen minutes, if you follow these each day. And it starts with the answer to the question I asked at the beginning, "How are you right now?"

Let's do an exercise.

What Can Happen in Fifteen Minutes?

Ask the next 8 people you speak to, "How are you today," and immediately write down their one or two word answers.

1) _____
2) _____
3) _____
4) _____
5) _____
6) _____
7) _____
8) _____

Most of the people probably said, "OK," "Fine," "Fair to Middle," "Fragile," "Average," "Hanging in There," and many other average to below average responses. Rarely will you get someone that says "Marvelous," "More Blessed than I Deserve," "Fantastic," "Fun," Fabulous," "Remarkable" or "Amazing."

Now, the second part of this exercise is when they ask you "How are you" You need to answer with the single most optimistic word that you feel would fit you on the best day of your life thus far. What word would that be: the day you got engaged, married, got a promotion, had your first child, watched your son hit a little league/high school/college home run, or your daughter graduated with honors from a challenging academic institution? What are some positive answers you can give when someone asks you "How are you today?"

1) _____
2) _____
3) _____
4) _____
5) _____
6) _____
7) _____
8) _____

The second part of this book is arranged in the following way. There are three core areas of every person's life that they need to focus on in order to have a fabulous life. Those areas are:

- Thoughts

- Feelings

- Health of your body

If you can manage those three areas of life, you can have a fabulous life!

Fabulous is not just a word, it is a lifestyle and it can be your new lifestyle with some effort and discipline. This section of the book will show you how to life that lifestyle.

Now I ask you again what is the difference between the person you want to be and the person that others see? Do they match and if not why? Take a leap of faith and ask others to describe you but only those you trust enough to give you an honest answer.

"We are what we repeatedly do. Excellence, therefore, is not an act but a habit."

-Aristotle-

What are your habits? Meaning what do you do repeatedly? As we have said before they ultimately determine your character. If you had to wear a name tag and had to replace your given name with three words, three descriptive adjectives, what three words would best describe you? Would others close to you say that you embody these three words every waking moment of your life? If not what if others' impressions of you were less than as positive as you see yourself; how do you change the negative impressions to the more positive words you are or want to be?

_____

_____

_____

_____

_____

_____

Do you have an attitude of gratitude and what does that mean to you?

_____

_____

_____

_____

_____

How do you show or share your gratitude every day?

_____

_____

_____

_____

_____

Make a list of everything you are thankful for right now. Write down something you are grateful for once daily without repeating one for 21 days. Then think of that thing you are so grateful for each night until you go to sleep so it is the last conscious thought of the day. End each day with thoughts that make you feel good, then start each morning with a simple affirmation. Make something up, use a favorite Bible verse, read the Bible until you find several verses you connect with in your life, use a poem that makes you smile, whatever works for you. BUT you must do this every day for 21 days to change out an old habit and start a new habit. Look at a baby picture, or a family vacation photo, of your son's first home run or your daughter's first ballet recital, whatever brings you joy. Write your Gratitude List write now, write here below. List the things/people or events you appreciate the most in your life and why.

_____

_____

_____

_____

_____

_____

Start reading your list every day when you go to bed and every morning when you wake. You start with one thing you are grateful for, then 2, then 3 then half way through the month there are 15 things on this list. Soon very soon you will begin to see the light, that fact that yes we all have struggles, we all have stuff in our lives as adversity skips no one's door. But on your list of things to be thankful for you do have a good life, there are many blessings, there is a great deal to be thankful for every single day. The more you focus on these the less you will have time for anything or anyone negative or draining. Think of yourself as a battery, one end is positive and the other negative, there is no in the middle. Do you bring more value to a relationship at work or at home? Are you a giver or are you a taker, you get to choose many times daily.

We must all work to focus on what we are grateful for and thank someone daily. Who have you told "I Love You" today? Stop reading this immediately and call or text three people and just say "I wanted to call and say I love you today". It is not a long conversation, so don't beat around the bush; make the call. Make It Now! Remember if you sat in a room with multiple people and everyone put their most personal problems on the table by the time you hear them all you'd gladly take yours back and go home. Be enthusiastic about your life.

"Nothing great was ever achieved without great enthusiasm."

-Ralph Waldo Emerson-

We all have so many blessings in our lives and those deserve most of your daily focus. So for those of you taking this seriously that you really do want to be feel and look fabulous and that you do not want to accept anything less; those of you that made that call or sent those texts, how do you feel right now, this minute, right after you gave out some love to someone unexpected but very deserving person in your life? Admit it, that it felt really well didn't it? What were the responses as I'll bet even though there are some party poopers out there, someone you called or texted was very appreciative and maybe even returned the gesture; how did that feel? You will find that when you look at life through dirty sunglasses it can look very cloudy outside. But when you look through rose-colored glasses everything is more beautiful—especially the roses themselves. Take less time focusing on the destination and more time to enjoy the journey.

Some people complain that a rose bush has thorns; few are so exceptionally thankful, grateful, and appreciative that a thorn bush has a rose. Which one are you; you do get to choose? The exact same situation (a rose bush) but framed from two opposite perspectives.

Look I am not saying this will make your problems go away, pay your bills, get your boyfriend back, or make you get along better with the in-laws. What I am saying is that the person you should be most concerned with is you. If you have the guts, ask some that you really care about if they feel in the midst of trauma, difficulty, or adversity, are you a positively driven individual that leans towards what is right or are you the one that leans towards what is wrong? You might be surprised by the answer if you ask it correctly and really do want to seek the truth.

Mental Mindset Management is very real and like any other muscle you have to work it out like you do in a gym. I find it ironic for example that many athletes spend 90%+ of their time getting bigger, stronger, faster yet they play a sport that most will say is 90% mental and rarely, if at all, work on these mental mindset skills. So whether you are an athlete or not, a mom or dad, a brother or sister, a doctor or lawyer, what have you done prior to reading this book to strength the muscle that drives more people to success and failure than any other, your mind and the belief system that fuels you daily?

"People are about as happy as they make up their minds to be."

-Abraham Lincoln-

Ask 5 people you know outside work to rank your attitude on a 1-10 scale. Then ask 5 people you know at work to do the same, tell them they will not hurt your feelings as being too polite will not help you at all. Remember this "All great performers aggressively seek feedback" as that is one of the best ways to improve.

How do you know what attitude or mindset you project until you make the time to ask others how they feel about you? It's simple, "John or Mary I am working on self-improvement and wondered if you could tell me the impression I leave with my attitude daily?" On a 1-10 scale with 1 being terrible and 10 being the very best attitude you have ever met in your life, where would you rank me? "Please be sincere and/or honest" as flattery at this point will not help me achieve my goal. Then be prepared to be slightly disappointed and also to say thank-you as without this feedback you will rarely get better.

What did they say?

_____

_____

_____

_____

_____

_____

"Of all the people on the planet, you talk to yourself more than anyone. Make sure you are saying the right things daily."

-Martin Rooney-

You should read this to yourself at least once daily/weekly, personalize the last sentence!

The longer I live, the more I realize the importance of attitude on life. Attitude, to me, is more important than education, than money, than circumstances, than failures, than success, than what other people think or say or do. It's more important than appearance, giftedness, or skill. It will make or break a company... a church... a home. The remarkable thing is we have a choice every day regarding the attitude we embrace for that day. We cannot change our past... we cannot change the fact that people act in a certain way. We cannot change the inevitable. The only thing we can do is play on the one string we have, and that is our attitude... I am convinced that life is 10% what happens to me and 90% of how I choose to react to it. And so it is with you... we are in charge of our ATTITUDES; it's the one thing in life we have total control of every single day in everything I do. I feel so blessed today about my life, my family, my...

Chapter Six:

Habits of Fabulous Thinkers

"If the only prayer you said in your whole life was, "thank you," that would suffice."

-Meister Eckhart-

As we learned in Part One, to master or control your negative thoughts, you have to plant good thoughts. Part of this is to be thankful or grateful about something every day. To do this, we suggest you take the 30-Day Gratitude Challenge. For the next 30 days, spend 15 minutes each day focusing on gratitude. Here are some very effective ideas to help.

- Keep a gratitude journal

- Pray and/or Meditate every day

- Tell someone why you are grateful for them / Say "thank you" more often

- Post to social media (Facebook-Twitter) something you're grateful for every day

What are you thankful for, what are you blessed to have in your life, what makes you smile? List some of those things here:

- _____

- _____

- _____

- _____
- _____
- _____
- _____
- _____
- _____
- _____

In addition to The30-Day Gratitude Challenge, take the "Pure Thinking Challenge."

"Once you replace negative thoughts with positive ones, you'll start having positive results."

-Willie Nelson-

Success coach Jim Fannin writes:

> What is a pure thinker? What's a typical day? This person has no negativity. None. A day like this is typically reserved for birthdays, anniversaries, Christmas, Easter, vacations, and other times where simplicity and positivity are common. This "pure" day is about living in the moment. There is no judging. No being a victim. There is no sarcasm. There is totally no frustration, impatience or anger. There are no eye rolls of displeasure. There are no dirty looks of discontent. There are no put-downs. It's a day where your "free will" sets you free from the shackles of what you don't want in your life.
>
> This day will take all of your self-discipline. You will need to commit to reducing your thoughts by 25-40%. You will need to focus. You must remain optimistic even when things happen that could hobble the optimist. And you will need to be calm and cool regardless of the oscillating circumstances, conditions, or situations. Lastly, this day needs all of your passion for simple living. Can you handle this at work, home and play? You are hereby challenged!
>
> Your assignment is to have one day of pure thinking. This is approximately 16 uninterrupted hours of positivity. Can you handle this? There will be challenges that will come in all sizes, shapes and forms. You will get cut off in traffic. You will have someone beat you to the "sale" aisle with only one product left. You will be bombarded by too many tasks and not enough time. Your mother will call and throw a wrench in your plans? Your kids could be unusually unruly. Can you do this? Which day would you choose to give this a try? Weekends? Football Sunday? Christmas Day?

When you start thinking negatively, immediately look around your environment for something you like and focus on it. Maybe it's a picture or your cell phone or your lunch. Think, "I really like this _____." This is the single best technique I know for changing negative thinking into positive thinking.

What can you do to be more upbeat more up tempo and generate more positive energy? Do you make perfect eye contact in every conversation, do you say thank-you to everyone. Are you are grateful about everything you have or do you complain about what you don't have? If you are a young person, do you say "yes sir-no sir" and "yes ma'am-no ma'am" to everyone older than you? Do you hold doors open for everyone? Do you put others' needs first?

Chapter Six Summary

As you begin Part Two of your journey from Fair to Fabulous, you are armed with the tools needed to complete your travels. These tools include the knowledge that with effort and discipline, you are well on your way to reaching your destiny, that of a Fabulous life.

While the first step in any planned vacation is walking out your front door and heading towards your vehicle, cab, etc., to begin your trek toward Fabulous, you must first walk away from a pattern of negative influences and thoughts. These roadblocks or potholes will only serve to slow your forward momentum. If you have ever been stuck in rush hour traffic or behind an accident on the interstate, you know that sometimes your speed may slow to a standstill and what appeared to be a certainty that you would reach a destination in time suddenly became a hurdle too high to scale. The same holds true for negativity's roadblock in your life. Fortunately, you have a choice – you can choose an alternate route.

By taking The 30-Day Gratitude Challenge, keeping a gratitude journal, praying or meditating on a daily basis, thanking others often, expressing gratitude to your friends and family and/or posting to social media channels, a process that may – in turn – spread gratitude should your friends follow suit and do the same, you will focus on your blessings and thus, your positivity. After you do this, will you remember the pothole at all? In *The Road Not Taken,* Robert Frost wrote, "*Two roads diverged in a* yellow wood... *And sorry I could not travel both... I took the one less traveled by... And that has made all the difference.*" Regretfully, those describing their lives as "okay," or "fair," or just "so-so" are often more prevalent in society than those choosing to be trendsetters or better yet, gods and goddesses of gratitude.

A few decades ago, a 14-year old girl lived in an apartment complex. She had many friends and responsibilities, like most teenagers, and surely like her friends. Unlike her peers, however, wrapped up in the latest Hollywood craze or fashion trends, she had heart. One afternoon, she noticed an older lady, struggling to haul her groceries from the trunk of her vehicle to a wheeled cart she used to transport them.

Surrounded by her friends, at the time, the girl heard nothing but snickers as the other teens ridiculed the woman, labeled her as mean, etc. Moved by curiosity, but also a drive of compassion, the teen offered to help the lady; help, which she accepted. Inside the woman's apartment, it quickly became apparent that her home had not been cleaned thoroughly for some time. Without reservation, the girl offered to clean the woman's home at no charge, just because it was the right thing to do. Despite warnings from the lady of how difficult the job would be, the eager teen would not take "No" for an answer. Over the next five days, two things happened: the 14-year old's friends continued to ridicule not only the lady, but also her, for choosing to help someone these teens dubbed "mean" and the lady, riddled by arthritis to where she could not have possibly cleaned the home herself, found hope for humanity and sparkling floors once again. After that week ended, the teen and the lady remained friends the rest of the lady's life. The lesson here is that young or old, big or small; anyone can choose to live each day with an "attitude for gratitude." If you live with an attitude for gratitude, you will likely develop a wonderful ability to tune out the negativity that may exist or surround you.

Before you can jump into action and take care of another's needs, you must take care of your own needs. If you strive to make each day a "pure day," free of negativity where you live in the present moment without judgment, sarcasm or playing the victim. Make a habit of living without anger, impatience, frustration, and lacking self-confidence. Any challenge you have faced has likely made you see the things you do not want in your life. Difficult people may have shown you how you do not want to live. By embarking upon this exercise of self-discipline, you will commit to reducing your thoughts by one quarter (25%) to two-fifths (40%), while remaining hopeful through times of hardship.

Live your passions while maintaining a peaceful sense of self. After all, when was the last time you practiced self-love and put your own needs before those of your family, children, friends or co-workers? You deserve to live in happiness, to embrace the blessings that surround you, and find a joyful purpose in life.

Have you ever noticed how happy you feel when you see a rainbow off in the distance? Have you ever stopped to consider why rainbows bring you happiness? For many, the rainbow is a sign of beauty after a rainstorm. Sure, a few also hope to find a pot of gold and fail to see anything other than the possible "monetary" reward at the end of a rainbow. Would your pot of gold be money? Or, would your pot of gold be illuminated by the joy you find in helping others, living life to the fullest, raising your family to the best of your abilities, etc.? Whenever you find yourself burdened by the personal storm, find something nearby that brings you joy. Let the pictures of your loved ones or pets, a special piece of jewelry that sparks a happy memory or even a touching piece of music with which you have a positive history be your rainbow, your personal go-to-guide of restoring the joy in life. If you are able to do this – to find the simple blessings in life, to appreciate the beauty that surrounds you, and to find seeds of joy that you can spread accordingly, you will not only be well on your way to living a Fabulous life, but you will help others to find their own sense of Fabulous too.

Chapter Seven:

Finding Fabulous Feelings

"Faith is taking the first step even when you don't yet see the whole staircase."

-Martin Luther King-

People with a fabulous life are able to manage their emotions. That's really the bottom line. If you feel great, no matter what your circumstance, you'll have a fabulous life. How else can we explain people who live in abject poverty, oppression, and other horrible conditions, and are truly happy? It's their ability to manage their emotions.

There is actually a movie on Netflix titled "Happy" in which the film makers go all over the world trying to find people that are truly happy. You will find it is not tied to wealth as many happy people are not wealthy and many wealthy people are not happy. If you have that service watch the film as the end result is that happiness has different meanings for different people in different cultures but ultimately all are a state of personal mindset.

Anthony Robbins calls this "managing your state" and describes an "emotional triad" that makes up how we feel. He says that feelings come from three things:

1. The way you use your body.
2. Your choice of words and voice quality.
3. What you focus on and believe about your thoughts.

We will get into #1 in the next chapter of this book. But this chapter will focus on #2 and #3.

"Energy and Persistence conquer all things."

Benjamin Franklin

Another way to create the most productive attitude can be found with athletes by creating your own version of the ICS, Ideal Competitive State. Even though not in any daily competitive scenarios at work or at home, sports is a great comparison to life. Many of us love our sports team and spend billions on jerseys and trips to professional ballparks and stadiums around the country. We can learn from them in many ways about mental toughness, leadership and the importance of controlling out thoughts/words/habits.

There are many very talented athletes that cannot make it to the highest level because they have little control over negative self-talk. Scouts will call it make-up and there are books, tapes and many tools to help them improve. But ICS or Ideal Competitive State is the best I have found thus far. The theory is when you are in your "ideal competitive state," you have feelings of energy, fun, confidence, courage, strength, relaxation, and fearlessness. Your "ideal competitive state" is then your state of being physically, mentally and emotionally which allows you to perform to the best of your abilities. It is a state of being when you feel your best and enjoy a challenge. It is the state of being that all successful athletes should practice getting to upon command. Learning to control your thoughts will help you reach your "Ideal Competitive State."

Can we at least admit together right now this minute that anytime you are attempting to do anything performance related if you are not in total ICS (Ideal Competitive State) of mind that you reduce your odds of success? Consequently, when you are at peak ICS you actually tilt the odd of success in your favor. There is now guaranteed system, there is no easy way to win, all you want is the odds in your favor opposed to stacked against you. What is the Ideal Competitive State? Is it your yearning to win on the ball field, in the office, with your friends or at home with your family? Or is it just hating to lose at anything you do? Like a school teacher that sends home a paper and writes on it 'capable of doing more'. What are you doing today with your life that you are capable of doing more? What are you doing at work that you are capable of doing more?

In Matthew 5:41 it says when asked to go one mile also go the second unrequested mile without expecting anything in return. Does this define you or your life right now as only you can choose to go that second mile without ever being asked. Are you the first or last on the practice field; are you first or last in the office every day? When asked to do something, are you the first or last to turn in that assignment to a professor? There are many things in life out of our control but all the answers to others' questions are yours alone and only you can decide.

For example would anyone describe you as someone that is "Chasing Excellence Every Single Day"? I believe it is not as much about wanting to win as it is refusing to lose or settling for second best. All Top Performers have an internal drive to be their best daily.

So what does a sport have to do with my life especially if I don't even like sports? Well I was also taught that Success Leaves Clues. If I can take something from one person or another and apply it to my life and make it better, why would I not jump on that process? In business, they call it best practices and companies try to share them frequently. So then there are certainly best practices regarding attitude and mind control. As such, why not try and apply them to your life and see if you can benefit? You can find your own "Fabulous." There are things in your life that make you feel good and inspire you to do better. We have all heard the saying find a job that you truly love and you'll never work a day in your life. Yet I have seen online surveys on AOL, for example, where more than 75% of those polled about New Year's Resolutions said they have a goal to get a better or new job in the following year. Odds are that you will be just as unhappy in a new job as this job or people. The same is true for those who quit on their marriage and find a new spouse as the one you have currently. You have to love yourself before you can love another and there are things about your job that you can find to make it better. You may not like hearing this but it starts with you.

"Fall down seven times, get up eight."

Japanese Proverb

Are you getting the theme yet, have any of these stories or examples piqued your interest? Even though all slightly different, they all share the same message. They all start with self-confidence and self-doubt. When you have a computer problem and you get online assistance, what is the first thing they say? Shut it down and reboot. You need to reboot yourself too and you get to do it every night. Start that positivity process with planting good thoughts nightly.

Rise Above It, what does that mean to you? People can be so rude. They can pick at you or complain or do just about anything to drag you down, especially when you are on top. Do you make the choice to bring them to you or sink to their level? The next time you are upset and say that so-and-so made me angry, you need to say they did something and I chose to get angry about it. Remember no one can hurt you without your permission.

"It's not the size of the dog in the fight; it's the size of the fight in the Dog"

Mark Twain

There are so many negative emotions they are tough to list but certainly anger, envy, hate, bitterness, being hateful, harsh vulgar language and other hateful things we say at times that we can never take back, the list goes on are all the negative end of the battery. Stay on the positive side of life's battery and "Rise Above" these emotions. I know it is hard and remember that anything easy is just not worth a damn, as hard creates progress.

Words and Voice Quality

In one sense, this relates to the exercise you did when asked "How are you?" The choice of words we use and the tone of our voice when we say it can have a dramatic impact on our feelings.

Try it! In the first exercise, say the following phrase like you mean it.

"Will this day ever end?" How did that feel?

Now, stand up, and say with all the enthusiasm you can muster, "I LOVE THIS DAY AND HOPE IT NEVER ENDS!" How did that feel? Quite a difference, huh?

So to manage your emotions, take 15 minutes a day and be very aware of the words you're choosing and the tone of voice you are using when you say them. When someone says, "How's your day?" your answer should be "FABULOUS" no matter what kind of day you are really having. Just 15 minutes a day can make a huge difference on the whole rest of your day.

Focus on the Fabulous

The third part of the emotional triad, according to Anthony Robbins, is what you focus on and believe about a situation. The way to change how you feel about a situation is to change the questions you are asking. You have to ask fabulous questions in order to have a fabulous life. What would I have to believe in order to feel this way? It will either be self-doubt (self-imposed stress or fear) or self-confidence, also self-imposed but now filled with confidence.

For 15 minutes a day, when you catch yourself asking the wrong questions like:

"Why did this happen to me?"   "Why is she acting that way?"

"Why does my life stink?" "Why am I so stupid?"   "Why am I always broke?"

Those are negatively biased questions. You need to rewrite the thoughts that you put in your mental garden. Change your default from why the negative into why not the positive. Buddha said "Peace comes from within. Do not seek it without". To me that means we seek inner peace and happiness and that clearly means we need more positive input and less negative input daily. Focus on what you can control and forget what we are unable to; you do control your thoughts.

Do you listen to inspirational brain food like Tony Robbins? You should, as we all need that kind of input as often as possible. Every day, in so many ways, we can tune up the muscle we call our brain by filling it with positive quotes, tapes, books, and videos. Check him out on YouTube, he is the real deal and helps so many people all over the world on their daily mindset management.

Switch the right questions to ones that are much more empowering.

"How this event a blessing in disguise?"

"How can I better understand her perspective?"

"How can I make my life better?"

"How can I learn from this?"

"How can I get additional resources?"

Whenever you start a question with the word "Why" you are automatically moving away from problem solving and into whining.

Instead, change the question to "How" and you'll immediately start feeling better. Once again it all starts with your thoughts. Clean out the negative fearful thoughts and replace them with more positive and fearless thoughts. This kind of self-talk ultimately determines your future both personally and professionally.

To feel stress, where does this come from? Your choice? Be courageous find emotions and feelings that are the opposite of fear. Center your focus on something that is positive and makes you feel good: such as a goal, a desire, or anything that you want to make happen. See it and then believe it and only then do you increase your odds.

When I listen to Tony Robbins speak, I immediately feel better about myself. Why? Because he has this ability to make you start believing in yourself. Seek him out, buy his books, listen to his tapes, watch him on YouTube, but go see him in person if you can. He—and other inspirational speakers like him—are able to help people like you and me to change our thoughts. You will not feel a connection with all of them; for me, however, Robbins speaks to my heart and my mind.

Growing up listening to Zig Ziglar and now Tony Robbins and watching movies just like The Secret, this is precisely how I exercise my brain and feed it the positivity it needs to get stronger. You too can do the same starting with this simple and fun e-book.

"Never go to sleep without a request to your subconscious."

-Thomas Edison-

What does this quote from so long ago mean to you? To me, it is the same as the foundation of this book. It is that the quality of your life and the quality of your thoughts. The premise of the quote is to go to bed at night thinking of something positive and in this case making a request of your subconscious mind that you want to accomplish.

"Optimism is the faith that leads to achievement.
Nothing can be done without hope and confidence."

-Helen Keller-

Some people pray before bed, while others meditate. You should focus on as many positive thoughts as you can both before going to sleep at night and then again as soon as you wake up the next day. Remember our conversations about planting seeds; in this case these are the mental seeds that we need to plan each evening and each morning so we know what will grow in the acre of earth that is our mind. What grows in your mind is whatever you plant each day. I pray every single night just as I get into bed asking for the strength to improve daily. What do you want to become, a better father, a better leader, a better son, a better husband. Until you know where you are going and what you want to be how will you get there if not focused on it?

"Over and over again, we lose sight of what is important and what isn't. We crave things over which we have no control, and not satisfied by the things within our control. We need to regularly stop and take stock; to sit down and determine within ourselves which things are worth valuing and which things are not."

-Epictetus-

I was watching Joel Osteen and he also talked about people being like computers thus when new we functioned perfectly. But sometimes a computer gets a virus and this virus now affects the computer software. You must work to clear out those viruses comparing our hardware to be our physical bodies and the software is like our mind. We must learn to delete any negative emotions. Do not listen to those trying to place eve more viruses into your mind like you cannot you will not, just hit delete he said. If you are going to reach your highest potential you have to become good at hitting delete. Do not let people contaminate your software as no one determines your destiny except you. His sermon was very powerful and very true as we can dwell on the negative or hit delete and focus on your beliefs. Think of your mind just like the software of your computer, turn off negative thoughts and reboot your computer like you can reboot your mind. We all need to work to stay away from things out of our control and to better focus on what you can control remember one fact we do get to choose our mindsets every single day.

He said do not let others determine your destiny by letting people say you can't do things, you're not smart enough, or put you down and you end up living in mediocrity. You must learn to develop discipline and focus on things that you are good at as only you decide what to focus on. Maybe some in your life can send negative thoughts and words, but only you choose to accept or reject them. Fill your mind with thoughts of hope, faith, and success. Focus on your seeds of greatness as people do not determine your destiny, you are in complete control. You need to work hard to program yourself to seek positivity and you will live a very successful life.

Dream big, see yourself doing something great and get out of any rut that will not allow you to rise any higher. Others do not program you, only you choose to accept a wrong mindset. The same is true that you can be confident and positive but you must reprogram yourself. Do not allow mediocre to become normal in your life. Just like we develop powerful mindsets we also create negative mindsets. Seek greatness and make excellence your new normal every day.

It does not matter where you come from or how negative others may have been around you, it starts by getting those negative emotions out of your mind. Get good at hitting delete when those thoughts come your way by stepping out of mediocrity and step into excellence. He said according to all the laws of aerodynamics a bumble bee cannot fly, but no one told the bumblebee and they fly just fine and have done so forever. What if that bumble had been convinced by someone that it could not fly? Fortunately no one communicated that to the bumblebee as nothing is impossible. Do not let your thinking limit you.

He has a daily devotional book called "I Am" that helps people properly program themselves daily. One Sunday if you are not feeling as confident as you need to be then just tune in to his program and get inspired you have nothing to lose and everything to gain. All of us need to plant more positive mental seeds and water them with self-confidence. There are so many resources available to us today that people like my father never had prior to the Internet. Some still found their own positivity but many did not, today there is no excuse for a lack of gratitude.

Chapter Seven Summary

People with fabulous lives manage their emotions without even thinking about it. Doing so has simply become like any other habit in life. It is something they do as involuntarily as blinking or breathing. These individuals have trained their minds to focus on positivity and you have that power within you as well. But it takes discipline just like taking time the read a book.

The happiness that exists in the world does not have anything to do with socioeconomic status and everything to do with each individual's mindset. Our feelings are born from the way we talk with ourselves and how we respond to situations. The manner in which you use your body, your choice of words, and your vocal quality correlates directly with your feelings. If you say "Oh I'll never get that promotion," you likely won't. If you say, "I am the best person I can possibly be and give my all to my job. I will get that promotion," you will put forth more effort to prove your worth to HR and your boss. Many companies choose to "grow their own" and hire from within a company as opposed to hiring from outside the firm. Why? Because by growing their own, a company allows their employees to develop the skills needed for the job and in turn, the company has invested time and energy in training, mentoring, etc. to teach an employee the ropes, if you will. An outsider with no experience working for the company would have to come in and learn everything from the ground up. Hence, those on the outside must work twice as hard to prove themselves as say; you would, already with a skill set that is acknowledged. The point to this scenario is that if you are positive and put forth an effort to achieve great things, you will achieve great things. You may not be able to control the timing, but you will find whatever success is meant for you in the long run and you will abide by the power of living a Fabulous life. People try to work out to get more physically healthy and thus we are asking you to spend fifteen minutes a day working on making your mental mindset both healthier and stronger.

When you think of success, what comes to mind? Hard work? Dedication? Understanding? Listening? Any realm of success leaves clues as to what has made an individual success. For some people, like the young writer dealing with critics that I referenced in an earlier chapter summary, considering the feedback of critics, but realizing that not everyone will like you, and thus continuing to pursue your passion despite this helped to build her confidence and her eventual success. If you take the time to observe happy couples or others that you know that are happy in their careers, marriages, communities, etc., there are undoubtedly clues for how and why these individuals have found success. Have they avoided drama by living a Fabulous life? Have they shown to work early and stayed late to get the job done? Look for any seeds that might help you to sprout more good thoughts and things in your own daily world.

Allow your life to re-boot. Restore your personal settings to a default of happiness and fabulous, while starting every morning with a blank memory card every day. As you prepare for a cross country vacation, you surely cleared your digital camera's memory card for any sight-seeing along the trek. The same applies to your daily life. Clear the memory card in your brain of all negativity and start each day fresh. Clear the card again at nighttime and sleep easier at night.

Always remember that you have choices. Not everyone will treat you with the respect that you deserve. That said, you have a right to choose your own definition of what you consider acceptable behavior. Your definition may be different than your spouse's definition, your neighbor's viewpoint, etc. but that is fine too. Remember that your journey in this life is yours alone to live and you get to choose how best to live it for you. Anyone can go through life allowing others to berate, abuse, chastise, or ridicule them; the strong, brave and committed to a Fabulous life decide to move mountains that stand in the way of their progress, that passionate about living a positive, fulfilling life. If you take 15 minutes each day to be more aware of your words and your tone when you say them, you will soon realize you are in better control of your emotions. When you have control of your emotions the results will always be more positive.

Questions that begin with "Why?" can lead to personal pity parties. If we choose to re-frame those questions as a call to action, such as

"How can I learn or grow from this experience?" you will find yourself with an inner drive for success and finding your fabulous!

The mental seeds you plant each morning and night are what will grow in your mind. But these thoughts or seeds must be filled with optimism and positivity. If you till your mind, reboot your thoughts, detour away from drama and other mental roadblocks, you will easily continue your smooth sailing towards a much more Fabulous life. Once you can figure out how to better manage your thoughts it will become like your own personal cruise control.

Chapter Eight:

Pay It Forward

The final area to focus on in changing from "Fair to Fabulous" in 15 minutes has to do with giving back. What can you do in your community to give back without expecting anything in return? When we were young, we all heard the saying it is better to give than to receive. But as young people we wanted to receive more than anything. The quicker you learn that it is much better to give than receive, the more fabulous your life will become.

Many of my friends and I have worked for years helping to raise funds for a local youth league, which was great fun. We also helped raise money to build a community park, and for a local chapter of the Miracle League which was amazing. A group of us assisted in Christmas parties for needy children and we cried happy tears. More of us packed back-packs for school kids who didn't want toys, but just wanted enough food to eat. I also cleaned up tables at a homeless shelter, which was humbling. I did all of these while being a husband/father and productive employee and these mean more to me than any material things we crave in our lives.

"You simply can't live a perfect day without doing something for someone who will never be able to repay you"

-John Wooden-

More than ever before our country's non-profits need your time and/or money. There are food banks, churches, homeless shelters, children's homes and hospitals, and facilities for the elderly. Sure, they always need money but many times it is more fulfilling and rewarding to give of your time. They need helping hands at so many different levels. If you try a few days of serving food at a homeless shelter, you will quickly see the things that you feel are problems are minor compared to so many others in need! You will learn quickly that absolutely nothing feels better or is more rewarding than helping so many of those unable to help themselves, young or old. You can learn that if you are not Giving you are not Living.

You can easily go online and locate a long list of needy organizations that are searching every day for helping hands. Nothing will make you appreciate what you have more than making a difference in the lives of others around you. Select a charitable cause you are passionate about and you will get so much more in return than you receive. Operation Smile, Big Brothers Big Sisters, Miracle League, Make-A-Wish Foundation, Wounded Warriors, and many more.

Giving back in addition to your normal daily responsibilities helps you keep balance in your life. Once you experience the needs of others you begin to appreciate your life even more.

Here are some options you can do to help transform your life from fair to fabulous.

- Create a small charity bake sale
- Get involved or start a walk-a-thon
- Start or join a local charity golf tournament
- Make a point to get involved in a children's shelter
- Give someone something of yours to someone that has always wanted it
- Stop by a children's hospital and read a book to a child fighting a disease
- Get a group and go by a home for the elderly and sing them Christmas Carols

As I have said paying it forward really means doing something for someone else without expecting anything in return. There are so many in this world live with slightly warped guidelines that every time they do something for anyone, they expect something in return. Yet there are so many opportunities to go out and make a difference that once you do so—like many others—you will get a rush from seeing that you can change the world one deed at a time. Especially when you realize you will get more out of these experiences than you could ever give to the person or organization you have become passionate about with your time.

Too many think it is about money or writing a check and while every non-profit needs more money, they also need worker bees. Thus, if you are in the position to help financially then by all means do so; but if not, then your time is a priceless gift to be greatly appreciated.

If you are a pet lover, volunteer your time at the Humane Society or a local dog shelter. Some of these just need people willing to walk the dogs and get them exercise. If the elderly touches your heart, then find a home and see if you can help. If you really connect with children, there are dozens of charities to help youth improve their lives. Find something to be passionate about and then make it happen. As more than anything else do something to make a difference.

"We make a living by what we get; we make a life by what we give."

-Winston Churchill-

This book is not about weight loss or getting a better job. It is not about having more friends. It is about "Taking Ownership" of your personal journey. Big and small, young and old, man or woman: there are few things we totally control. Yes, we all have many obstacles in our lives and some are very unfair. Have you ever watched a video about Dick Hoyt? He and his son were on the ESPY's this year and when you see his journey through life and what he has done for himself, you will know what I mean when I say despite the present circumstances you still get to choose. Make a decision right now, when someone asks you how are you today?

Take notice of those around you and attach yourself to the most positive people you know. With a better mental mindset, you can't help but end up with a better job and more friends and a happier healthier life? Take charge, use your choice with your voice, and you can be Fabulous today. Shake off the bad and focus every morning and night on the blessings in your life. It is almost impossible to be grateful and pessimistic at the same time. Be grateful today...

Our youngest son plays college baseball and as a result I have invested in an over the top camera that shoots 10 frames per second and has a lens so large I need a small suitcase to carry it to the games. On occasion, people ask me to take a picture or two of their sons. Recently while at the Florida Summer Collegiate Baseball League (I highly recommend the FCSL) game, a Mom from the opposing team asked if I'd take a few pictures. Her request reminded me of a quote:

"And whoever shall compel you to go a mile, go with him two"

-Matthew 5:41-

I had several options: just say no thanks, go ahead and take a few and e-mail to her, or really do way more than she requested or especially suggested. In the quote above, she asked me to do something and I decided to do more. I took almost 100 high speed action shots, I placed them on a CD to give to her and while at it, I was inspired enough to Photoshop several, grab the team logo from their website, and make her a smoking hot collage of his efforts that day.

When I see her or hear from her if she says to me 'what do I owe you', (I have done this many times before) my response is going to be please "Just Pay It Forward" and then next time someone asks you to do something just say yes and then do twice what is asked of you.

Imagine if she asked her son to mow their lawn and he went out and mowed his house plus the elderly neighbor's yard. (Someone does that for my 82 year old mother, pretty cool) Imagine at Christmas for each 3 gifts you buy your child you buy at least one for a homeless child or orphan. Imagine at Thanksgiving when you cook a huge meal for your family, you also donate an equal amount of food to a local food bank or shelter. The list is endless of what you can do if you choose to live it by the one simple quote. Try this at home with your spouse, with your kids, with your friends, at your job, or at your church. They say the traffic on the second mile is very light and it may not be the whole world that will do it but it can be your world.

Chapter Eight Summary

The last stop on your journey from "Fair" to "Fabulous" in 15 minutes focuses on giving back. What can you share with others? What unique gifts do you possess that would be beneficial to another facing their own difficult circumstances? If you make the decision to be a leader and not a follower, a trendsetter instead of just accepting the "norm "others may feel is appropriate, you will not only live a fabulous life but also show others that a fabulous life is possible for them as well. Living your daily life as a giver, selflessly sharing with others with no expectations will place you at the apex of enjoying a much more Fabulous life!

The gift of giving back or paying it forward is far reaching. Whether you volunteer your time to support charity or offer goodwill to those less fortunate, putting forth the initiative of sharing your wealth of blessings and talents with others takes only a little time while offering rewards that will be reaped for a long time to come. Further, if you have ever been helped through a tough time and currently find yourself in a better situation in your life now, paying forward to others those kindnesses you received in a time of trial spreads gratitude and goodwill with those who can now most benefit. Helping others who are less fortunate not only spreads kindness and humanity, but serves to remind you that any problem you may be facing in your life is minor in comparison to what others go through daily. You may find many online charities and support groups in need of assistance. Choosing one or a couple different organizations that interest you will help you to maintain perspective and a balance in your life.

Strive to change and better the world, even if only one person at a time. Your support of others does not have to be monetary; others will always be available to give money to aid charities in need. Walk-a-thons or charitable 5K runs, and volunteering your time in others ways to bring awareness are just as beneficial to any charity and are often overlooked in the name of monetary donations. Every non-profit needs check writers and worker bees, make your choice.

Own your journey in this world. Be mindful of those in your inner circle and pay closest attention to those who are positive. Learn from that, feed off their positive energy and live happily, each and every day. Tell the bad times and any negativity in your thoughts or your life to take the proverbial hike and focus on your blessings. If you are struggling to see the blessings, start with admiring the morning sunrise. Each morning's sunrise is a sign you have been granted another day. What is more Fabulous than that, focus on everything you have to appreciate daily?

If you get into the habit of doing twice what is asked of you and only ask that others pay it forward in the future, fabulous will flourish and so will you! Remember everything we do or say has the potential to affect the whole; imagine how powerful that is. As the pace and fullness of modern life serve to isolate us from one another, the contact we do share becomes vastly more significant. We unconsciously absorb each other's energy, adopting the temperament of those with whom we share close quarters, and find ourselves changed after the briefest encounters. Everything we do or say has the potential to affect not only the individuals we live, work, and play with but also those we've just met. Though we may never know the impact we have had or the scope of our influence, accepting and understanding that our attitudes and choices will affect others can help us remember to conduct ourselves with grace at all times.

When we seek always to be friendly, helpful, and responsive, we effortlessly create an atmosphere around ourselves that is both uplifting and inspiring. Most people rarely give thought to the effect they have had or will have on others. When we take a few moments to contemplate how our individual modes of being affect the people we spend time with each day, we come one step closer to seeing ourselves through the eyes of others. By asking ourselves whether those we encounter walk away feeling appreciated, respected, and liked, we can heighten our awareness of the effect we ultimately have. Something as simple as a smile given freely can temporarily brighten a person's entire world. Our value-driven conduct may inspire others to consider whether their own lives are reflective of their values.

A word of advice can help others see life in an entirely new fashion. And small gestures of kindness can even prove to those embittered by the world that goodness still exists. By simply being ourselves, we influence other's lives in both subtle and life-altering ways. To ensure that the effect we have is positive, we must strive to stay true to ourselves while realizing that it is the demeanor we project and not the quality of our wondrous inner landscapes that people see. Thus, as we interact with others, how we behave can be as important as who we are. If we project our passion for life, our warmth, and our tolerance in our facial features, voice, and choice of words, every person who enters our circle of influence

Conclusion

Well, there you have it. You now know everything you need to know in order to help transform your life from Fair to Fabulous if you commit to fifteen minutes work every day.

Everything we do in our life either takes us closer or farther away from our goals. Ask yourself if the way I am feeling right now is this helping to move me closer to the person I want to be or further away. If they are negative hateful angry emotions, Let Go and Let God.

Remember the acre of earth tilled, fertilized, watered, with sunshine? What grows in that acre of earth and in your mind is precisely what you plant. You choose what to plant every day in your mind and thus then with your actions. All of us have that negative self-talk to deal with and as I've told our sons, there are only two ways to feel about any situation or opportunity. Approach them with total Self-Confidence or Self-Doubt and they both start with "Self". We do get to make that choice every single day in every single circumstance.

I "highly recommend" you watch the movie *The Secret*, but don't be like so many I have met that come away with thought like you can't dream about a bike and then have it show up on your front porch. Instead watch this movie and keep a small note pad and come away with 5 simple thoughts you feel you can apply to your life. This movie has so many great speakers and the Law of Attraction is very real and has been talked about many years before this movie was produced. If you are so inclined Google the law of attraction and you will see it is not only very real but been around throughout many civilizations. It's pretty simple the more positive you think the more positive things that you attract; conversely the more negative you think the more negative things you see and attract. We have been on this; it all begins with your thoughts so I hope the process sinks in for you. Read and live by Matthew 5:41 always do more than asked.

If you are a baseball player, should you go to the plate worried about striking out or confident that if the pitcher has to throw three over the plate; then you only need to hit one to be successful. There are no guarantees that positivity will make you hit the ball but it is proven to give you an edge and in life, all you want are the odds tilted in your favor. A slight advantage you need that starts once again with self-doubt versus self-confidence. Think of a battery: there is the Plus side and the Minus side; there's no in between. You choose to be either one or the other. The coolest part is we do get the make that choice every day. Ask yourself right now, which end of the battery are you? Are you a daily energy giver or an energy taker? Do you feed the demon on one shoulder or the angel on the other daily? At home do you bring more to your family or do you take away? At work you are either part of the solution or you are the problem. On a sports team you are either making the team better by adding value or you are taking a uniform away from someone that would work harder than you. There is no middle ground; just being OK is for those taking the easy way out. In the book Good to Great, remember that Good is the enemy of Great because as long as you are OK with good you will never be willing to pay the price to achieve greatness. Seek personal excellence every day.

Try using a gratitude journal, or a vision board, or listening to tapes and reading more e-books as we all need positive rewarding fulfilling brain food. In the computer world, the phrase was coined Garbage In-Garbage Out. Once again we restate that your body may be the car, your legs the wheels, your arms your skills, your brain the engine, but the type gasoline you put in the engine determines the performance. Your personal fuel starts with your thoughts.

"The mind is everything, what you think you become."

-Buddha-

I hope and pray you will cut and paste or highlight the sections in this e-book that touched you like they inspired me when I was taught these lessons. There is no one size fits all but remember everyone needs positive reinforcement. There are millions of dollars being made every day on self-help books, seminars, tapes, and movies. The reason they all do so well is because the vast majority of people you will meet, work with, play a sport with, or have a relationship with are mostly glass is half empty people. You can change that and we can start right now.

Being negative is easy, staying positive throughout all life's challenges is hard. For example you and your wife and/or girlfriend can have a great month, flowers, dinners, and walks on the beach, literally 29 days of almost bliss. But if on the 30th day, you drop the ball, forget a special occasion, say or do something wrong, it can be as though the prior 29 days of excellence never happened. That's the most destructive of the negative forces in life; the negatives can wipe out all the positives in a second. Negativity can kill a relationship; it can cause trust that took years to earn to disappear in a moment. Focus on what you are grateful for every day as we all have so much to appreciate.

Why is it that in life there is no scorecard or no credit for doing well? Why does the news media always talk about a school bus running off a cliff and 2 students dying opposed to focusing on a tragic accident where 38 students survived? We know the majority of our population buys newspapers or watches the news on TV that focus on traumatic events. Be the one in your family to start a new more optimistic direction, and it starts with your thoughts.

"Do not go where the path may lead, go instead where there is no path and leave a trail."
-Ralph Waldo Emerson-

What does this quote mean to you, as to me it's pretty simple. Young people drink because they see others drink and smoke because others smoke. No one has ever been born and later used their first words to say, 'may I have a smoke please'? You have to choose to be different, choose to run off that negative news, to cut negative people out of your life. Choose to stop planting negative thoughts in your head. You—and only you—can make this happen. You have to take complete responsibility for your own daily mental mindset management. Make up your mind that no one can upset you without your permission.

Make a decision and a commitment right now to make a change in your thoughts. Decide you deserve more success, a better life, better health, to lose weight, to stop smoking, to spend more time with your family and less time at work, to take more vacations. Go tell your wife/ husband how much you love them and what a huge part of your life they are and that you can't live without them. Take your wife/girlfriend/ significant other flowers today for no reason at all and sign the card, Just Because... Decide that you deserve it and you are on the path daily from Fair to Fabulous in fifteen minutes each and every day!

**"Our greatest glory is not in never falling,
but in rising every time we fall."**

-Confucius-

I hope you review this book often and highlight the chapters that speak to you as these life lessons have spoken to me over the past thirty five years. You can change your life, you can redefine your goals, you can create a better outlook, you can enjoy the journey by seeing the best in everything and everyone, and you can go from Fair to Fabulous in fifteen minutes a day if you choose to read some of this book daily!

In summary, I want to share with you a weather forecast that forever changed my life. One night late, when I wasn't really paying attention to the TV, the news anchor said "Ladies and Gentlemen tomorrow is going to be either partly sunny or partly cloudy depending on your perspective on life." That really stuck with me and I have made the CHOICE to at minimum be partly sunny even on every rainy day and fabulous on every other day. Why when they say it is a 30% chance of rain, people start to worry about getting out their umbrellas? Why not say there is a 70% chance of sun and get out tanning oil and your sunglasses?

Be the change you want to see in the world

"Mahatma Gandhi"

What change do you want to see in your world, guiding our children with don't tell me show me and this only happens when you find ways to show your gratitude by giving back. Change your default by finding something right in everyone and every thing, the minute you are able to do this your life will change forever. Live not by complaining about things you see that you do not like, live by giving everything you have to everyone you know, it will come back 10 fold and nothing is more fulfilling that helping others without expecting anything in return.

Giving back can change your life forever but you will never know what it feels like until you reach out there and give it a try. I know many such individuals that were very focused on building a bigger house, driving a nicer car, and launching their careers they had little time to volunteer. Then once he took the leap of faith to experience raising money for a kid's park or helping to grow a private school or giving children a Christmas to remember or visiting a boy's home that they left their jobs and sought out a career with non-profit organizations.

When you look back on your life you have to ask what is your legacy going to be? What I men is we all raise families, we all have jobs, we all try to mentor others along that journey. Find a friend or a family member or someone at work that volunteers on a community service committee and ask them what they get from their involvement. Each of us are driven by something that will touch your heart. Some love to get involved with children's charities, some are passion about the elderly, while others go to the SPCA as they love animals. I could easily see my wife taking in stray dogs as she is the dog whisperer in our home.

We all read about the professional athletes in many sports as some do nothing and then others really go above and beyond. Kirby Puckett from the Minnesota Twins brings other professional baseball players from all over the country for a weekend fund raiser for Children's Heart link and amazing organization helping kids that need heart surgery. In the end just ask yourself this, when it is your time tom depart what have you done to make this world a better place than you found it, the answer to that question may just move you. One organization that moves me is the Wounded Warriors program, on a recent flipping last Vegas show they refurbished a house and gave it to a wounded warrior, I cried as they changed his life.

It is 5:38am and I am in a hotel the day after finally finishing this book and for whatever reason I woke up and wanted to finish the conclusion of this journey. Five years ago, it came to me that I wanted to share the knowledge of so many great leaders before me that shared this information with me. Then, three years ago, I looked at my goals and saw that I was letting my life get in the way of living this dream. On March 20th 2012, I was blessed with the opportunity to start this book and here it is July 28th, 2013 and its done then edits took until July 20th 2014.

I want you to know that when searching for publishing houses most asked what were your goals and mine is not to make money on this book. I start a brand new job August 2nd with Wyndham Worldwide and could not be more excited about that new opportunity. My goal for writing this book is the hope that unlike me it doesn't take you 30+ years to figure out the lessons I have shared with you. To learn that no one can hurt your feelings, make you mad, or put you down without your permission. To learn that the only goal you are incapable of reaching is the one that others tell you that you cannot do and you agree with their thoughts and let them become your thoughts. Athletically speaking coaches (the very people that should tell every young athlete to follow your dreams) tell kids they are too short, too slow, or that they are not athletic enough to plat at the next level. Sadly, some agree and give up what they love. As it also is in life, people tell others what they cannot do instead of reiterating that anyone can do anything they want if a person wants it bad enough and is willing to exchange something for it, because they never accomplished it themselves.

Success in life is never about your success, it is about how many people you took with you on that journey. We should all seek to be the change we want to see in the world. Do not read the newspaper or watch the news and get so filled with negative feedback that you feel you cannot make a difference. An older man was walking the beaches after a terrible storm and there were starfish and other sea creatures washed up for miles along this stretch of beach. He came upon a young girl picking up as many starfish as she could and watched her walk them down to the seaside and throw them back into the water. Innocently he said to her, "young lady there are way too many of these for miles and miles on this beach as one person you simply cannot make a difference in all of them". She picked up another walked down to the water and tossed it as far as she could and looked at the older man and said, "I just made a difference with that one."

Know that each of us can make a difference with our lives one person at a time. Part of my prayers has always been about being grateful to every military service person for the freedom they provide us every day that so many take for granted. Of course I pray for my family and many other things every evening and every morning. But part of my new daily prayer will be that you are a starfish that has had the sea of life blow you up onto a beach and that I am that young person writing this book hoping to make a difference with you. That right this second I am picking you up and throwing you back into the ocean to have a second chance at a fabulous life. Be grateful that I did not listen to that kind of gentlemen who thought maybe a really nice person has given up on his or her chance to make a difference.

Believe that all of us make a difference. Believe that you can lose the weight you need, you can get the job you deserve, and you can find the spouse that will love you unconditionally for the rest of your life no matter your current age. Appreciate your children, love your spouse unconditionally, show respect for your parents, and find greatness in your chosen profession. Make a commitment to go out and lead by making a difference in the world starting right now.

Now it is time for me to say to you, Thank-You for taking time to read these words. You are in charge going forward; do not let anyone else determine your state of mind or your belief in yourself. Believe no one except those that love you unconditionally. Stay away from negative input and the media and don't let them get you wound up and stressed out about the bright future you have ahead of you. Stay away from what you cannot control. Focus on the things in your life that you can control and place most of your energy and efforts on those things daily.

Read more inspirational books from great speakers like Tony Robbins. Go online and find people like Brian Cain who has devoted his life to teaching people how to become their own Mental Mindset Masters. Follow Zig Ziglar on Twitter or listen to the Secret on CD's in your car. It is all out there for you and it is not coming to you now as you must take the first step, you must want to change you must want to get better. You can go from Fair to Fabulous every day.

On the last page of this book is a simple poem that has been thoughtfully crafted especially for you, tear it out or make a photo copy and place it somewhere in your home and read it every day for the next thirty days. You can do this; I believe in you, do you believe?

I just watched Stuart Scott's speech from the 2014 ESPY awards when he won the Jimmy V Foundation award and cried like crazy. Challenge anyone feeling bad or finding things to complain about in their life to watch this video soon to be on you tube. There are so many opportunities for you to see there are so many with such deeper challenges than you have yet they still find inspiration and ways to take time to inspire others like he did tonight.

The only real change that will happen in your life will start the second you finish this book and take action. Success definitely leaves clues and all the other famous people quoted have left us those words of wisdom to help us make changes to make our lives better and to enjoy during our lifetimes. Pick three of those quotes and write them down and read them every single day for next month and then send me an e-mail at: FairToFaublous@aol.com

Find 2 or 3 parts of this book you most connect with and focus on those immediately. The only way I am able to "Pay It Forward" is if you devote 15 minutes a day every day for the next thirty days on your own personal journey from Fair to Fabulous in 15 Minutes! You will make a choice now, a choice to make a change, a choice to get better, a choice to do something, and yes if you choose to do nothing that too is making a choice.

Recently my sister was at my mother's house and found my father's Bronze Star with a V for valor and his Purple Heart that actually had the metal pieces taken from his body attached. I wanted to publically thank him for his service and thank him for being the inspiration of my life~

I look forward to hearing from you soon!   Wayne L. Rickman

"Thoughts-Words-Actions-Habits-Character-Destiny"

Today I know begins with each and every "thought",

I am going to be optimistic as nothing will make me distraught.

Please be the wind beneath my wings so I can fly high like a bird,

By being extremely attentive to what I say
with each and every "word".

When confronted I need to be careful to
respond and not have a reaction,

For what quickly crosses my lips will
ultimately be put right into "action".

When my positivity rules the day it can and
will multiple just like rabbits,

As these things we say/do/feel ultimately
become our personal "habits".

In the long run these daily efforts will pay off of that I am very sure,

As responding to life's challenges will always
build upon my "character".

I know it takes work and will take a great
deal of extra effort from me,

But in the end this daily discipline will become my mental "destiny".

Wayne L. Rickman

April 26, 2013